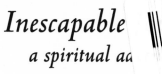
Inescapable

a spiritual ad

Inescapable Journey
a spiritual adventure

CLAUDE SAKS

HEARTSFIRE BOOKS

AN IMPRINT OF HAMPTON ROADS PUBLISHING COMPANY

For information write:
Heartsfire Books
c/o Hampton Roads Publishing Company, Inc.
134 Burgess Lane
Charlottesville, VA 22902

Or call: (804) 296-2772
FAX: (804) 296-5096

If you are unable to order this book from your
local bookseller, you may order directly from the publisher.
Quantity discounts for organizations are available.
Call 1-800-766-8009, toll-free.

ISBN 1-57174-034-1 (paper)
ISBN 1-57174-033-3 (cloth)

10 9 8 7 6 5 4 3 2 1

Printed on acid-free paper in Canada

DEDICATED

to Yeshe Tsogyal

Author entering Yeshe Tsogyal's cave.

ACKNOWLEDGMENTS

The events in this story are all true, to the best of my recollection. All names are real except for those of four people who requested privacy. My tale would not have unfolded without the help of the spirit world. Particular thanks to Michael Morgan, channeler of Yokar, as well as to Yokar himself, an ascended master who is connected to the stellar mind and who was an Atlantean priest and scientist at the time of his incarnation on Earth.

Thanks to Steven Nickeson, Sara Held, and Gail Vivino for their editing, and to all the other friends who have offered their suggestions. Much appreciation to Marcia Keegan for the cover photograph. Thank you to Juan Li for his drawings and photographs, and to David Carson for his help on my journey and his wonderful foreword. I am also very grateful to Hampton Roads Publishing Company for taking over in the middle of the project.

Most of all I want to thank my golden lady, Emer Featherstone, for her tireless efforts in correcting my grammar, typing the many drafts, and wrestling with various computer programs.

I acknowledge with thanks *Body Mind Spirit* magazine for publishing part of "The Messenger" (Chapter 2) in their January/February 1991 issue.

CONTENTS

FOREWORD

I met Claude Saks several years ago when I was living in Taos, New Mexico. I was impressed by his esoteric knowledge, his formidable business accomplishments, and his spiritual dedication. I have sojourned with him in the hills of New Mexico while he connected with his future encounter in Tibet. I have seen his power of concentration, his willingness to encounter the unknown, and his commitment to truth within self.

In modern America the spiritual drive is often expressed in a consumerism of ecstasy. We think that if we invest in the right workshops, books, cassettes, or even the right teachers, we will achieve peak experiences that will permanently transform our lives.

Claude knows that the valleys and the plains are vaster than the peaks: they offer more fertile environments for the steady cultivation of spiritual life. Claude pays his dues. He knows that the spiritual life requires honest, tireless effort and that it dares us to deal with the ordinary—the inescapable ego strivings of daily life—as well as with nonordinary states and energies. His book explores the balance—sometimes precarious—between ordinary and nonordinary, between light and dark, between outer and inner, between our everyday consciousness and what is hidden from our commonsense consensus perceptions.

My own teachers often spoke of the deeper mysteries of life. They saw that I was asleep to reality. They said that most of my convictions and stubbornly held beliefs were demented lies that I hid behind, and that I was afraid of the true possibilities. Today I enjoy the possibility of at least 186,000 interpretations of reality per second.

Our consensus conditioning leads us to narrow, habitual definitions of reality that we consider "normal." Teachers throughout the ages have attempted to wake us up, to rouse us—a race of sleepwalkers and soul-dead beings. We must wake up, they tell us. We must remember who we are. To do that we must exert great effort. We must break out of the prison of consensus mind and be born again. We must die and disappear and live once more in truth.

I am grateful to Claude Saks for making the effort to shatter the unexamined life and for offering his experiences of truth at a deeper level.

This book is about spirit and the exploration of the light and shadow sides as we walk the sacred trail of life.

Perhaps Claude's work will lead you to a confrontation with your own higher purposes. Perhaps his example will lead you to climb your own spiritual mountain.

I hope so.

David Carson
Co-author, *Medicine Cards*
Carrizozo, New Mexico
March 1995

PREFACE

*One can fool life for a long time, but in the end it
always makes us what we were intended to be.*
— Andre Malreaux

This book is not for the person who has all the answers,
nor the person who is content with money and all its
material representations. This story, my story, is for the
seeker; for the person in search of the divine that is within
the darkest self or on the mountaintop.

My purpose in writing this book was to provide a guide
to a personal transformation in the form of actual examples,
rather than in the form of a philosophical discourse. I
wished to write in concrete terms about energy and the
divine in everything, and in doing so to provide an adventure. I have included within this story my various spiritual
methods and meditations, including specifics that cannot
be found in writings anywhere else at this time.

Included also are addresses where my teachers and I
can be reached, for those who would like to inquire further
into the spiritual paths that have been touched upon in this
book.

Inescapable Journey

a spiritual adventure

1 A Matter of Heart

Get rid of your minefields, and
come out of your bunker.
—Dr. Morano

I was in a different space—frozen in one spot. It was September 1, 1977, just prior to Labor Day weekend, and we were warming up for a mixed-doubles tennis match in Montclair, New Jersey. My wife Bette moved with grace and determination on the other side of the court, her auburn hair flashing in the early morning sun.

"Bette, could you come here please?" I requested.

"What's the problem?"

"I don't know. I can't seem to lift my racquet. I have a pain shooting down the underside of my right arm."

"What kind of pain?" she asked. Her blue eyes narrowed as she looked at me intently.

"I don't know. A dull aching pain. I just can't lift my arm. I have the same pain in my left arm and moving up my throat under my chin. And my back aches."

The color drained out of Bette's face; even her freckles seemed pale.

"Come on. We're going home. I'm calling the doctor."

"Hold on. Maybe I should just rest a while." My six-foot frame was limp, and I leaned on Bette.

"No. I want you to come now."

"Okay, okay."

After the call, Bette took me directly to the emergency room of Mountainside Hospital. Arrogance, control, possession, and laser focus had been my trademarks. Success in the international commodity world required concentration and unwavering dedication. What was about to unfold was not part of my program. When we arrived at the hospital, the staff had been briefed. I was still in my tennis clothes and felt awkward. I was immediately put on an examining table. The attending nurse started to attach an intravenous tube to my arm. I jutted my chin testily.

"Is that necessary? I really don't like intravenous needles. I'm liable to faint."

"Standard procedure for any cardiac symptoms. If you need to faint, go ahead. We have smelling salts."

"What do you mean cardiac symptoms? There's nothing wrong with my heart."

"Sir, you are manifesting all the classic symptoms, and the doctor has told me to proceed accordingly."

I was in disbelief. How could I be having a heart problem? I was strong, I was in control, and I had a lot of things to do! The company I had started in 1972 was one of the largest coffee importers in the United States and one of the top five worldwide. I was on the fast track—I worked hard and I played hard. I overate, drank, and smoked. I felt that my financial and material success would protect me from any unpleasantness.

"Who is the doctor in charge?" I asked the nurse.

"We've paged Dr. Horowitz. He's a cardiologist and he's doing his rounds. You're lucky. I think he's one of the best young doctors in town."

"Is he board certified?"

"Yes, and a graduate of Stanford Medical School, which I assure you is one of the best."

At this point Dr. Horowitz walked in. "Mr. Saks, how are you feeling? Do you have chest pains? Are you feeling muggy?" He was thin, long-legged, bespectacled, and soft-spoken.

"No chest pain, some discomfort under my arms. Yes, I do feel muggy, but I was playing tennis. Sorry, I smell like a gymnasium."

"Don't worry about that. We've seen a lot worse. Here, put these pills under your tongue."

"What are they?" I asked.

"Nitroglycerin. They will dilate your arteries to help the blood flow."

"Why? My blood flow is fine."

"Mr. Saks, let me decide that."

I took the pills.

"When will I be released?"

"We're going to keep you here overnight for observation."

"But there's nothing wrong with me. I want to go home."

"Mr. Saks, it is very possible you are undergoing a mild cardiac infarction right now. I want to make sure we are doing everything necessary for your safety."

I could not process the idea that I was having a heart attack two months before my fortieth birthday. It was my first brush with death.

Dr. Horowitz turned to the nurse and gave her instructions. From then on things moved without my help. I was transported to the CCU, the Cardiac Care Unit, and hooked up to every imaginable monitoring device. I was angry. I had large coffee positions and open currency contracts that needed to be concluded, and I didn't have time for this nonsense. Then came the blow to my ego. The blood test came back and the enzymes indicated I had indeed had an infarction. Dr. Horowitz did not believe there was any serious damage, but he wanted to keep me in the CCU for a few more days. I was receiving glimpses of my human vulnerability.

By midweek I was moved to a private room and began to receive visitors. When my friends came, we joked and laughed, pretending life would be the same when I left the hospital. I played along, but my deep self sensed a major turning point. My body had been speaking to me; I just had not listened. Finally, God had kicked me in the chest, in my heart center, to focus my consciousness on something more important than my business.

Dr. Horowitz wanted to keep me under observation for

another couple of days until I stabilized. He explained he wanted to perform an angiogram.

"What's an angiogram?"

"Basically, we run a filament up the arteries to determine where there might be a blockage."

"What do you mean? What blockage?"

"Most likely your heart attack was caused by a blockage in one or more of your arteries, causing a lack of blood and oxygen to your heart muscle."

"How is an angiogram performed?"

"Usually we make a small incision in the large artery of your groin, and then work up from there."

I was feeling faint. Much later, I would get some insight into my tendency to faint. I would discover that I fainted in situations in which I lost control. To avoid experiencing that, I would check out—I would faint.

"Okay, okay," I responded to Dr. Horowitz's description. "I don't want to know. Once the angiogram is done, then what?"

He explained that, depending on the results, I might be put on medication or undergo bypass surgery.

Two days later, Bette and Dr. Horowitz walked in, both looking rather somber. Bette sat on the side of the bed and held my hand. In a flat, measured tone she said, "Claude, I have something important to tell you. First, I want to say everything is going to be fine, so don't get upset."

I tried to act chipper and said, "What's up?"

Dr. Horowitz responded, "While riding his bicycle, your son, Eric, was struck by a car, but he's okay."

"My God! What do you mean by 'okay'? Where is he?"

Bette put her other hand on my arm and squeezed gently.

"Claude, calm down. Dr. Horowitz and I have the situation under control. Eric has some injuries, but he's been checked over and will be fine."

"What injuries?"

Bette described Eric's broken left leg, now in traction, and his broken left wrist in a cast. I inquired about his head. She assured me that he had not had a concussion and had been checked over by an eye, ear, nose, and throat specialist.

"Where is he?"

"He's here, two floors down."

"Can I see him?"

Horowitz interjected, "Yes—we will wheel you down."

"I can walk. I'm perfectly fine," I responded.

Bette put a stop to that. "Claude, please do as Dr. Horowitz says. We'll wheel you down to Eric's room. Then you can walk a bit."

I was wheeled down two floors. Then I stood up next to Eric's right side. His brown hair was disheveled and his dark eyes peered up at me. His right eye was black and blue. His left leg was three feet up in the air in traction, his left wrist in a cast already covered with his friends' signatures. He had a few scratches here and there, but he was smiling. I just stood there holding Eric's hand, fighting back the tears. I leaned over and hugged him, my eyes watering, then tears sliding down my cheeks. Bette joined the embrace and we all cried.

Where had I been all the years of Eric's life? He was a fine young man of sixteen, and where had I been? I sat on the edge of his bed. He did not want to think or talk about the accident. He was having nightmares. We talked about his interest in art and in particular his desire to be a filmmaker. I listened. I really listened. Yet I could not translate my feelings into words, and my brain was not assimilating his words. Everything was jumbled: my empathy for Eric, and my concerns about my own health, my business, Bette, and my other children. After a while Dr. Horowitz came back and insisted I go back to my room. Eric and I both needed rest.

A few days later I was back home, on transderm to dilate my blood vessels. Dr. Horowitz insisted I stay quiet. In two weeks Eric came home in a hip-high cast. Bette arranged for him to live in the ground floor family room where he could wheel about. I spent a lot of time with

Eric and my other children, Marc and Claire—but there was a distance between us. Marc was now thirteen, blond and tall for his age. Claire was eleven. Her sadness at our illnesses showed through her blue eyes. I had been so busy building a financial empire that I had been unaware of my lack of connection with my own children. How could I not express my deep love and feelings for them? I needed time.

I started to move around a bit but was still under strict orders not to do business. I called the office but no one would tell me any of the problems; in any event, the company had begun to seem distant and unimportant. At that time I did not understand that I was being called in another fashion—to switch from being a material warrior to being a spiritual warrior. My first lesson in yielding had begun.

I started going up stairs on a regular basis and kept denying to myself that I had chest pains. However, the fact was that I did have pain. Finally I broke down, told Bette, and called Dr. Horowitz.

He suggested I have an angiogram at Mountainside the next afternoon to evaluate what steps to take next. I was reluctant; the Montclair hospital was not equipped to do heart surgery, and my gut told me the procedure should be done at a full-service hospital. Horowitz wanted to think about it, and within forty-five minutes he called me back. He had spoken with a cardiologist friend at Columbia Presbyterian in New York, and they had arranged for an angiogram the next day.

Bette rode with me in the Montclair volunteer ambulance to the Bronx, and I was processed through the Columbia system. The next afternoon I had the angiogram. The cardiologist was great. We spoke the same language—he was quick and to the point:

"Mr. Saks, your angiogram shows that your left descending anterior artery is 90 percent blocked. I consider you in a very critical condition and recommend that we do bypass surgery immediately, as soon as we have a free operating theater. One of our best surgeons is standing by and he will come and visit you shortly."

"What about a second opinion or alternative method?"

"In your case there is no time for a second opinion. You are a walking time bomb. There is no alternative solution for your blockage."

"Okay, I hear you. Let's do it."

I was starting to understand that my lifestyle was going to have to change. But how? I needed to know all the facts. I asked the doctor if he had any suggestions on books to read. He recommended two: *Type A Personality and Your Heart* and *The Relaxation Response.* An operating theater would not be available for several hours, so my business partner, who had come in to lend support, volunteered to go get the books. After searching half the Bronx, he returned with the two books. It was now 6:00 P.M. The surgeon checked in with me, reviewed the risks, and assured me the best team was standing by. I rifled through the books. As I anticipated, they made it clear that my whole life had to change. My personality had to change. *I* had to change. What I felt at that time was not a fear of death, but a concern for my lack of conscious emotional connection to my family. At the same time my intuitive or higher self knew with a clear certainty that I would not die.

The orderly finally rolled me to the operating room at 10:30 P.M. I was put on the operating table and told to breathe deeply as a mask was lowered on my face. I do not remember meeting God while I was on the operating table; but from that time on, my laser focus shifted. I became a spiritual warrior.

I have vague recollections of being cold in the recovery room. The next morning, in the Intensive Care Unit, tubes coming out of my nose and solar plexus, I focused my attention on Bette. I smiled and said, "It's hard to get rid of a bad weed."

She relaxed, figuring I would make it. I was lucky. I needed only one bypass. Within three days I was walking feebly around the hospital. Within a week I was released and wheeled to a waiting car. I was extremely weak, and the cardiologist explained that it would be quite a while before I regained my strength. I had lost a lot of blood. He had refused to let the surgeon give me a transfusion unless the operation became critical. (In retrospect, in light of the AIDS crisis, his decision was a blessing.)

Back at home, fear set in. I became conscious of every little pain or abnormality. Now that I had life, I was concerned with dying or being permanently handicapped. I was not equipped physically, mentally, emotionally, or spiritually to accept being in a weakened condition.

Just being alive, in and of itself, seemed important to me; action and doing no longer held the same attraction. Being alive, just being, was okay. Slowly, I got in touch with myself. I spent a lot of time with Eric, who was still convalescing. When Marc and Claire came home each day I spent time with them too, trying to make up for the years when I had not been around. A dramatic change had occurred in my life, but I still lacked the means to be in touch with my children beyond a superficial level. I loved them deeply, yet I could not express my feelings.

A few weeks passed and I started to spend half-days at my office. A limousine picked me up at 9:00 and brought me home at 3:00. I plunged back into the problems at work, where everyone's adrenaline flowed. Telephones rang constantly, coffee prices jumped up and down, but I lacked the motivation to act. I let others pick up the phone. I was not comfortable in the office.

On November 18, 1977, a month and a day after my operation, Bette held a surprise fortieth-birthday party for me. My friends brought a lot of silly gifts and I laughed a lot, did not get drunk, did not overeat, and thoroughly enjoyed myself without the excesses of past occasions.

My partner made a toast to Bette, thanking her for her strength throughout Eric's and my crises and congratulating her on keeping the whole family calm and together. I listened, realizing that I should have been the one making the toast. Why was it so hard for me to acknowledge

Bette's help, her abilities and strength? I was still unable to express my deeply felt emotions.

I decided to address the needs of my body and mind. Without my conscious decision, my spirit followed. In order not to revert to old patterns, I realized I needed to find extra time for myself. I signed up for a monitored cardiovascular-exercise program three times a week and joined a transcendental-meditation group in the hope of calming down and lowering my blood pressure. I stopped smoking and my weight dropped to 185 pounds from 215. I began to get in condition. The seeds of change were germinating.

I decided to go see Vincent, a psychic who had become a friend of mine. He had wavy black hair that was always well groomed, and deep, dark eyes with a soft yet penetrating quality. We met at his apartment in a modest building in New Rochelle. We sat in his consulting room. After a few pleasantries Vincent looked at me intently.

"Well, I think the time has come for you to start on your spiritual path," he said. He went to his bookcase, pulled out a book, and handed it to me. It was *The Mysticism of Tibetan Buddhism* by Lama Govinda.

"Vincent, what is this? I don't know a thing about Eastern religions."

"I know, but you've started transcendental meditation, which is the first little step in that direction. I know you don't have an interest in religion, but my sense is that spirituality will become important to you."

I listened to him when he used the words "my sense," because I believed he was inwardly seeing or hearing actual events. He continued, "If you really are going to take a new path and you want to become a more open human being, then you need to arm yourself."

"What are you getting at?"

"I think you should consider seeing a psychologist—a person who is also on a spiritual path so that he can guide you along the bumps."

"Thanks, Vincent. What am I, nuts?"

"No. You're growing, and I'm just trying to facilitate

your path, but without pointing out the hurdles and obstructions. You need to find those for yourself and work through them."

"Okay. Any suggestions as to a psychologist?"

Vincent mentioned Dr. Morano, a friend of his.

I decided to meet Dr. Morano at his home office in New Jersey. Like Vincent, he was of Italian descent, with thinning hair, a tightly cropped beard, glasses, and a rounded, soft appearance to his body: not soft in the sense of being flabby, but soft in the sense of not being outwardly muscular and aggressive. He looked like a panda bear. I kept well in mind that underneath the panda's soft exterior is an aggressive and tough animal.

"I'm flattered that Vincent recommended me. So what brings you to see me?"

"I want to change my personality."

"Oh—something as simple as that."

"I realize that's a simplified statement and that it will take time."

"Why do you want to change your personality?"

"Basically, I'm a type 'A.' I'm extremely intense in all my undertakings. I want to control everything in my surroundings. I plan my objectives five years—sometimes ten years—ahead, and then try to fine-tune events to suit the outcomes I want. In doing that I seem to miss everyday living, particularly my relationships with my children and my wife, as well as those with the many other people who are close to me."

"Are you prepared to put some serious work into this process, and are you ready to devote time? Maybe years?"

"Yes."

And so started my process with Dr. Morano.

While I was undergoing psychotherapy, I read numerous books about mystical teachings and became intrigued by all their ramifications. I did not understand everything I read, but my interest was awakened. I wanted to know more. I kept up my TM (transcendental meditation) practice faithfully, five times a week. I found my mind more alert and conscious of what was around me. Slowly, I started to understand my family. I became more responsive. While beginning on this spiritual path, my business continued rolling along. I verbalized my feelings of love to my children, which in turn helped them to express their feelings. Bette and I talked of my need to get more deeply in touch with myself, both through psychotherapy and the spiritual path. I could not explain to her what happened to me in meditation except that a deeper knowing seemed to be present. My urge was to pursue the way of spirit. She responded, "Honey, don't bring your rage to succeed to your desire to be spiritual. My feeling is that you need to follow your intuition and not your head."

I did not appreciate her comment until years later, after I had read book after book and my rational intellect had brought me no closer to what I sensed existed in the ephemeral. My gnosis would eventually manifest, but only after years of inner work.

My spiritual search intensified. I wanted something more than going to church and listening to a sermon, or doing transcendental meditation to lower my blood pressure. Tibetan Buddhism, which I read about first, required me to absorb too much information and I did not know how to start. I began to investigate the most direct of Buddhist practices—Zen. I located a *zendo* in New York's Soho district, ten minutes from my office. I walked in cold and spoke to the abbot, explaining that I believed I wished to practice Zen. He had one of the young volunteers show me how to sit: legs crossed, preferably lotus style (which I never could master), back straight, picturing the vertebrae lined up like a string of pearls held by an invisible thread coming through the crown of my head, with my chin slightly tucked in, chest and shoulders relaxed. I sat on a round, six-inch-thick meditation cushion called a *zafu* so as to form a triangular support for my body—my main weight distributed on my knees and perineum, the lowest point of my torso. I started to understand that the purpose of meditating was not to relax but to develop heightened internal awareness. I had to center my mind to meditate.

Once a week after work I would go to the *zendo* and sit. I would do twenty minutes of sitting, ten minutes of silent walking, and then another twenty minutes of sitting. I also continued my TM. Gradually I found myself more centered. Issues floated into my consciousness while I sat: issues of arrogance and greed, related to my business deals. I drove a Masarati, owned a large racing yacht, and went out to all the finest restaurants. These outward manifestations conflicted with my inner meditations. I was still building financial walls of protection that represented emotional barriers of safety. There was a dichotomy between my business passion and my spiritual passion. I discussed these issues during my sessions with Dr. Morano. Years would pass before I understood that everything is energy, that everything is spirit, and that my intuitive decisions in business were building blocks for my future path.

I was a slow learner.

One day Dr. Morano simply shouted at me, "Don't you understand you had a fucking heart attack, a *heart* attack! You're supposed to open up your heart *chakra*, open your compassion. Get rid of your minefields and come out of your bunker. The world is all right!"

With the help of Dr. Morano and my spiritual search, I started to understand. I became more accepting of my surroundings. With this, my urge to get out of my business grew. I began to see that my continued need for the excitement of big deals and money was counterproductive to my very being. I sold the company in January 1980 but stayed on for five years as a full-time employee. Instead of twelve- to sixteen-hour days, I now worked eight to ten hours per day. I was very well compensated. I trained new traders and managers to take over the company. I slowly turned over my international travels, which used to take me to Africa, the Far East, and Central America, to the new deal-makers. I gradually withdrew from the excitement and adrenaline of the international world.

My feelings were all mixed up. On the one hand I was

glad to have collected my money, and I felt secure; on the other hand I felt my child—my business—had left home. Bette and I discussed it.

"Sweetheart, this is what you have been aiming for. You pulled off one of your best negotiations and it was very intense. It's normal that you should feel a letdown when it's completed. Relax. Give up some of your responsibilities and devote more time to your family and yourself."

She was right. I resigned all my titles as well as my position as chairman and director of the board. I was shedding the business world. I sat in meditation in the *zendo* twice a week and I sat at home every morning before breakfast.

Still, I felt I was not moving forward on my spiritual path. I discussed the problem with Dr. Morano during our sessions. He said, "Listen Claude, Zen ultimately may not be your path, but issues are coming up when you sit. Psychoanalysis is the Western approach to the true self, while the Eastern approach is through meditation. Both are valid. You've chosen to do both at the same time. That may be accelerating the process."

"I hope so."

I got a call from Marc, who was now a freshman at the University of Colorado at Boulder. We talked about the courses he was taking. I was proud of my six-foot-two, blond, second son.

He told me, "I've joined an ashram and the swami is great."

I thought, "Holy shit, he's joined a cult. How am I going to save him?" Instead I said, "What does that mean? How can you be in an ashram and still be in school?"

Marc explained that he attended meditation and spiritual classes only in the evening. The swami was a strict disciplinarian about attending school or working; he taught that the ashram was not a place to hide from the world. Marc recommended a few books to me, including *Spiritual Cannibalism* by Rudi, who had established a Kundalini Yoga lineage in the United States. Reading the book, I learned about the practice of using positive and negative experiences as fuel for our psychic-spiritual digestive systems. I decided to go and visit Marc.

Bette and I flew out to Colorado. Marc, his usual joyful self, clear-eyed and smiling, met us. We drove out to Eldorado Springs, outside Boulder, to meet the swami. Surprise! Swami Sambavananda was a large, happy American man with dark curly hair and big smiling eyes. He had grown up on a Pennsylvania farm and became involved with spiritual work after hearing Rudi lecture at his college in Ohio. I took an immediate liking to him as we sat on his sunlit terrace with snow still on the ground.

"Swami, I am pleased to meet you. I was concerned that perhaps Marc had joined a cult."

He smiled his broad, embracing smile. "Our ashram is not a place to come and hide from the world. Rather, it is a place to do serious spiritual work. We are having a beginners' meditation later this afternoon. Why don't you join in and see for yourself?"

Bette responded, "Well, I've never meditated. I don't want to disrupt anything."

"You won't disrupt a thing. In fact, we'll have an instructor give you a few pointers before we start so you'll feel comfortable."

"Thank you, I'd like to do that."

"What about you, Claude?"

"Yes, with pleasure. I've been sitting Zen for a while so I'm accustomed to sitting. May I ask how you became a swami?"

"Certainly. I studied with Rudi, that is, Swami Rudrananda. At some point he told me I should go to India and do some work with the present head of the lineage, Swami Muktananda. To make a long and complicated story short, Muktananda made me a swami."

Marc had sat quietly throughout the entire conversation. When the bell for meditation rang, he led us to the meditation hall. He felt more comfortable letting another student explain the sitting posture and give us a mantra to use during meditation. A mantra is a combination of words used in rhythm with one's breath to still the mind. We sat through beginners' meditation for about twenty minutes and then chanted for another fifteen minutes. Afterward, I went up to Swami to thank him. He gave me a big hug and I could feel his love surround me. I knew Marc was in good hands.

Back in New Jersey, I read other books and found out more about the previous head of the lineage, Swami Nityananda. I felt a conflict developing within myself between Zen, which involved sitting totally in quiet, and Kundalini Yoga, which seemed to work with moving energy through the body. Some days I would sit Zen style; other days I would try to visualize the movement of energy through my body. I began to get tingling sensations at the base of my spine and in my sex organs. I could not tell if the sensations were figments of my imagination or actual openings. It was only years later that I understood that Zen is based on the grounding principle. The opening comes naturally when the aspirant is ready, an explosion of energy that transports him or her to higher realms.

For now, I was leaning away from Zen and trying Kundalini Yoga, but I had no teacher. I needed to resolve my dilemma. The break came when I decided to get more information on the sex chakra—the chakra of creativity and the human life force. I had walked into East West Bookstore in New York and asked the attendant for some help. He suggested I might want to read some books by Mantak Chia.

"Is he a Kundalini Yoga master?"

"No, he's a Taoist master. I think you might be astonished by what the ancient Chinese knew. The Taoists don't call the body points 'chakras,' but they use similar points to those used by the Hindus, the Tibetan Buddhists, and other yogis."

"Okay, thanks. I'll give it a try."

I rummaged around the Eastern religions and philosophy sections and picked up *Awaken Healing Energy through the Tao* by Master Mantak Chia. I was in search of a practice that moved energy, as in Kundalini Yoga, and calmed the monkey mind, as in Zen. I leafed through Master Chia's book. "This is it!" I exclaimed, standing in the middle of the store while everyone stared at me. And then to myself I thought, "This guy's got the answer." I decided I needed to find Master Chia and learn from him.

After several inquiries I found Master Chia giving courses in Taoist meditation in an old, rickety building in New York's Chinatown. This was early in 1983, before he developed a big following. I went to his classes and sucked up every word and practice. At the end of a two-day intensive course, he sat on top of a table in front of the class and, simply by making eye contact with each of the participants, transmitted energy. I literally felt a shock hit me and energy start flowing. I knew deep in my core that I had found my path.

What I loved about Master Chia was that he had no interest in being a guru or swami in the traditional sense of requiring awed reverence from his students. He simply wanted to teach and guide; it was up to the students to practice and develop from within themselves. One of Chia's favorite sayings was, "If you get it, you got it."

The initial sessions with Master Chia involved opening the outer energy channels of the body. These channels flowed down the front part of the torso and then up the spine to connect through the tongue. This circulation of energy was called the "microcosmic orbit" in the Taoist practice. The practice started with a "smile down," which involved breathing in a golden, embracing mist or energy and smiling in and down to oneself, through the nostrils and third eye (mid-eyebrow). This was to calm the mind and prepare a heightened internal awareness. The practice was to smile down the energy to each organ and limb. Once the mind settled, one could start the microcosmic orbit, always finishing the circulation in the belly center to avoid excess heat creation. (I would strongly recommend that any aspirant buy Master Chia's books on the various meditative formulas and follow up with classes with a certified Taoist teacher. The only practices reviewed in this book are those that cannot be found in other books at this time.)

The microcosmic orbit was the answer to my search. The circulation of energy hit blockages in my back, again bringing up my issues of control and my unwillingness to be more fluid in my everyday life. After the tantric or (as I define it) energy flow part of the practice, I sat quietly, my mind settled, and experienced a deeper sense of self and the divine order of the world around me.

In talking with Taoist friends, I found that people had different reactions or blockages in their bodies that needed to be burnt through. Some people experienced heat or tingling sensations in various parts of their bodies, while others had very subtle energy-flow feelings.

As I progressed in my spiritual path with Master Chia I learned the more advanced and deeper alchemical formulas of transformation. They were alchemical in the sense that they energized not only the physical body but the spiritual body. I found my connection to everything around me becoming a living reality. After opening my outer channels, Master Chia taught me how to open my central thrusting channels, which I could then use to send energy out of my body to explore my connections to astral energy.

I found this process particularly intense during Taoist retreats, when the collective energy of the group seemed at times like a rocket. During one such retreat, I experienced my energy body merging with that of a woman participant on the astral plane. I experienced complete joy and an orgasm on a spiritual level that cannot be explained on a physical level. The movie *Cocoon* comes closest to describing such an experience.

One of the practices that I learned was how to recirculate my sexual energy upward, instead of into a physical orgasm, so as to experience godly union with a partner. Unfortunately, many people have bought Chia's books for the express purpose of extending sexual activity without understanding its use on a higher plane. I found that it was always important to emphasize the beginning, or microcosmic, practices to ensure my energy and spiritual growth.

It was through Master Chia and his summer retreats that I formulated my views about spiritual teachers and their followers. The attendees and followers of Chia came from all walks of life: they were lawyers, actors, accountants, healers, and homemakers. What they all had in common was an ego. All these people came to understand that there was more meaning to their lives on Earth than that obtained from their professions or occupations. They had intentions to grow and transform into more conscious spiritual beings.

Many paths teach that students must have ultimate devotion to their teachers; this can work provided the teachers, in turn, are totally devoted to their students' spiritual growth. So when I meet spiritual teachers, I not only look at their teachings and motives, I also look at their students. If they are what I call "woo-woo," if they dress in the latest spiritual fashion and talk about loving the world, but have not taken action by rolling up their sleeves and helping, I walk away from those teachers. They are nothing less than spiritual bloodsuckers draining their followers' energy to boost their own.

By 1987 I had completed all the meditational formulas taught by Master Chia. I was deepening my practices, yet I had a sense there were other pieces to the puzzle I needed to learn in order to continue my spiritual journey. My path was to take a leap forward through unexpected occurrences.

I would find that the road of spiritual growth to the ultimate attainment of the thousand-petal lotus flower, as described by the Buddhists, involved rooting in the mud and muck of the shimmering pond. I would encounter physical death again. The preparation for and resolution of that encounter in the rarefied air of Tibet would bring on further deaths—of parts of my ego, emotions, control, attitudes, and way of life. I would learn how to engage fear.

2 The Messenger

Now it's all in God's hands.

From the time I had been twenty-nine years old, I had
been a high-stakes gambler in the biggest world casino:
commodities. I retired in 1984. Three years later, in October
of 1987, my friend John Feuer called and asked if I would
help him negotiate a coffee deal in India. John's intensity
matched my own. We were both born under the sign of
Scorpio. At six foot three, he was taller by three inches.
He had thinning blonde hair, piercing blue eyes, and a
long, energetic gait. At forty-nine years old, I was older
by a dozen years, with thinning hair and a full, dark beard.
My eyes were hazel-gray to black, depending on my mood,
and I matched him stare for stare.

The players in the coffee deal included a large Park
Avenue barter company; Tata, the largest private company
in India; and the Indian government. John felt he needed
my expertise and offered a very attractive consulting fee,
which I accepted. A proviso of the fee was that I would
not have to travel outside of a fifty-mile radius of New
York City. After I had retired, I had continued trading for
my personal account and now had a lot of currency contracts
in the futures market. I did not want to undo them in order
to travel. Besides, I had no interest in going to India. I
had traveled extensively through Central and South America, the Far East, and Africa. I had dealt with many Indians
who were coffee shippers out of Africa and felt a hypocrisy
in them—an inconsistency between their spiritual beliefs
and their business methods. John assured me that all

negotiations would be done on Park Avenue.

I was looking forward to being part, once again, of the wheeling and dealing involved in large contracts. Deep within me I knew the process would be different, for I was very different. My spiritual path had brought a clarity that I could not describe in everyday terms; perhaps this clarity was a result of my higher intuition. So I approached the negotiations with detachment and amusement.

Our meeting was held in the barter company's elegant mahogany offices located at 37th Street and Park Avenue. We sat around a coffee table in comfortable armchairs and couches. Introductions were made. Philippe, the power partner, was a tall, heavyset, cigar-smoking man. Efrom, the analytical partner, was short, thin, and nervous.

Philippe opened the conversation by addressing John. "I want to make it clear from the outset that the contract will be between you and Tata," he said. "They are heavily into steel, motorcars, and other industrial manufacturing. They want to diversify one of their divisions into coffee. We are friends, and we do a lot of barter business with them all over the world, including the Eastern Bloc countries."

John listened quietly. I decided to jump in and get to the nitty-gritty. "Am I to understand then that all business, good and bad, will be between John's company and Tata? That you are putting both parties together because of your friendship with Tata?"

Efrom jumped in. "No, no. We expect a $75,000 finder's fee from you up front, plus 10 percent on all shipments with a minimum $150,000 guarantee overall."

I looked at John. First he got pale, then his color started to rise. His blond hair bristled on his red scalp. "This is not what I was led to believe when this meeting was set up," he said. "You told me you needed an outlet for Indian coffee to help a friend and that you would facilitate a mutual contract."

Philippe said, "Come on, John, you know these big international deals don't come about by the sweetness of our hearts."

I cut in before John blew his stack completely. I was clear. I knew how to proceed. "Listen, let's calm down," I said. "First we need to define our parameters. Perhaps then we can find a meeting ground." I raised some questions: How much coffee were we talking about? A thousand tons a month? Would they guarantee the performance and quality? Historically, Indian coffees were overpriced on the international markets because the official convertible rupee rate was fictitious. The only companies that had been successful had been able to get the Eastern Bloc or internal black-market rate. I continued, "Will you guarantee us the lower rate of exchange? If you can give us satisfactory answers to these questions, then perhaps your fees might be justified!" I felt the energy shift. It was palpable.

They were taken aback. Philippe recovered and said, "We only want to act as the introductory broker and get our commissions. It's up to you to get all the details from Tata."

"There is no one in the coffee business who is going to pay you up front for castles in the sky," I said. "Telex to Tata and get the answers. Then we can talk."

Efrom said, "We can't put these types of questions on telex, because all communications are monitored by the government. As to our fee, how would you propose working?"

I knew I had him. All they had was an introduction and nothing else. I was not about to let John pay them a cent until he had a clear contract with Tata and all the answers. I said, "The only way that John could pay you a commission would be on the basis of each shipment completed, with a time period of no more than two years and a cap of $150,000. That is, provided he obtains a clean contract with Tata with all the answers."

I was smiling, but my eyes pierced into Philippe's and my tone was flat and final.

Philippe sat back in his chair as if to capitulate. "Okay, I think that could be workable, but we don't have the answers. You would have to go to India and work with Tata face to face."

I shook my head and looked at John. He smiled and said, "I'll double your fee if you come to India with me."

Something in me said I needed to go. "Done deal," I said and I shook his hand. We would make good traveling companions. During the trip, we would play great-humored games of ferocious backgammon.

Shortly before leaving for India, in the first week of December, I chaired the last board meeting of the year for an AIDS research foundation. After the meeting I mentioned my upcoming trip to Vincent, also a board member. He asked if I would deliver a personal letter for him to Sri Sathya Sai Baba, an avatar, a saint of saints whose ashram was located in Puttaparti, near Bangalore. I agreed and said he should give me a call when the letter was written.

A while later I received his call. Vincent's voice was soft as velvet over the phone. "Claude, my letter is ready. Would you mind also delivering one for Finn?"

Finn was a dedicated helper with many of the AIDS projects.

"Really, she knows about Sai Baba?" I asked.

"Oh yes, she spent a week at his ashram a few years ago. She feels she has a psychic link with him and that he communicates with her in her dreams."

I picked up the letters and read a book about Sai Baba before leaving for India. The story did not impress me. The author wrote mainly about Baba's ability to materialize gold rings and other physical objects, and I felt any evolved human being could do this. My main interest was his connection to spirit and whether I could feel and experience that connection.

A week later John and I were on our way to Bombay for our connection to Calcutta. We landed in Bombay at 1:30 A.M. The temperature was just bearable. We checked into the hotel and I immediately went to my room. I showered, donned pajamas, and called the front desk for a 10 A.M. wake-up. Then I slipped into bed, but sleep would not come. I tossed and turned, my body clock a mess. I decided to sit up and meditate. I breathed in and smiled the energy through my third eye, letting the familiar warm, tingling sensation spread. I circulated the energy through my channels to move into the higher energy planes.

Then my entire body blew up. I was taken over by energies beyond my comprehension. Golden light filled my entire being—every inch, every square millimeter, every molecule of my body. I felt I was expanding beyond the size of the room, filling with energy and in total ecstasy. Sobbing with absolute joy, I let everything go; I surrendered. I smiled inwardly, the warmest, deepest, happiest smile of my life.

Through this haze and halo the figure of a man appeared—as real as any man I have ever encountered. It was Sri Sathya Sai Baba. He was short, wore an orange robe, and had an Afro hair style; he had gentle features and a warm, all-knowing smile. He said, "Welcome to India. I have been expecting you."

My ears rang with his soft tones. More golden light and warm, embracing energy flowed around me. The seconds passed. Or was it hours? I was lost in time and space. Eventually "monkey mind," as the Zen teachers call it, took over and reasoned that I should get some sleep for the negotiations later that day. I tried to merge with the light and energy, but I had no control over it. It floated all around me, in me, became part of me. It was me. I stumbled to bed.

I could not sleep. An even greater explosion of golden light and ecstatic energy poured from my eyes onto my cheeks, beard, neck, ears, and hair. I traveled to other dimensions, dreamed, perhaps slept.

The phone rang. "Good morning, Mr. Saks, it's 10 A.M."

The energy was gone; the golden light was gone. The pillow was like a sponge from all my tears. I took another quick shower, dressed, and felt totally refreshed, alert, clear, and ready to travel and negotiate. We headed out to our Calcutta flight, the heat bearing down on us, and smells and dust emanating everywhere. Although my surroundings seemed surreal, I felt on familiar ground. Every moment was part of my being, my consciousness, my greater reality.

We landed in Calcutta in the afternoon and were met by Aspi, the lead man on the coffee project. As we stood in the midday heat waiting for our car and luggage, I assessed Aspi while he talked to John. He was of medium height, rotund and joyful, and spoke clear, fast English. I was the consultant, so all the conversation was directed toward John. I stayed in the background and observed, interjecting my contributions only when needed.

A beggar walked up to us. He was scruffy, disheveled, with only one eye and one hand. I figured his parents had cut off his left hand when he was a child so he could enter the begging profession. I wondered about the eye. I was about to give him a few rupees to get rid of him when I thought better of it. I wanted to observe how Aspi would handle the situation.

Aspi was explaining the program. "I will drop you off at the hotel so you can freshen up. The car and driver will wait for you and will bring you over to our headquarters. We will have cocktails with the chairman to discuss an overview and then proceed to dinner."

The beggar kept sticking out his hand for alms. Aspi casually turned to him in the middle of his talk, said a few words in Hindi, then continued his explanation as if he had been uninterrupted. "Tomorrow morning the driver will pick you up at 8:30 to bring you to our office. I have left my calendar open for our talks. I have booked the three of us on the 2:30 flight to Bangalore."

I looked over at the beggar, who was standing motionless and erect next to Aspi. Aspi caught my glance and said, "I told him that if he was quiet I would give him a few rupees when I'm finished. I have scheduled two-and-a-half days of talks with the government coffee people. That will leave us Saturday afternoon and Sunday to conclude our business and visit the surroundings. Does this meet with your approval?"

"Yes, that sounds fine," John said.

At this point the car and driver pulled up. Aspi paid the beggar, our luggage was loaded, and we were on our way downtown.

Calcutta was like a frenetic anthill, with traffic jams, absolute gridlock, honking horns, car exhaust, and pollution so thick you could cut the fumes with a knife. My eyes stung from the toxicity, heat, and oppressive humidity. We were chauffeured to the best hotel in town, hidden behind thick walls, quiet as an oasis in the midst of cacophony and pandemonium.

At Tata headquarters we were introduced to the chairman, who was quite congenial. An exploration of the potential business was held over cocktails, and I realized that negotiations would be with Aspi. We set a very positive tone for negotiations, which continued through an excellent Indian dinner and into the following day. All the questions we had raised at the Park Avenue office were answered. John's contract would start at a thousand tons of coffee a month, to be reviewed in six months. His arrangements with the barter company were his business, and the contract would be directly with Tata. Rupee exchange rates were none of our concern; Tata would respond to John's pricing and take care of their own internal affairs. They would guarantee all quality and shipments, provided we helped them set up a system in Bangalore. At the end we all shook hands, a deal done. We then flew to Bangalore, the coffee region of India, to evaluate the situation firsthand.

By Saturday afternoon we had accomplished our business in Bangalore, and we set out to locate Sai Baba. Several inquiries led down blind alleys. Finally, late in the afternoon, we located Sai Baba's agent, who booked his public appearances, and asked him about the possibility of setting up a meeting for me.

"You don't understand, my dear fellow," the agent replied. "Sai Baba is a great saint. Millions of people— poor, rich, and famous—want to have an audience with him. That is not possible. Sai Baba will only see people he himself picks out of the crowd at the ashram. You are in luck, however. He is not at his Puttaparti ashram, which is a long journey from here. He is presently at his private residence at Whitefield, only an hour's drive from Bangalore. He has a small ashram there. His devotees come there at 9:00 in the morning to receive his blessing and see him. So if you leave Bangalore no later than 7:30, you should arrive there in time to see him."

At this point the agent stopped his singsong explanation and looked up at me intently. He continued, "Wait, I have a good feeling about you. Come back tomorrow morning and pick me up at 7:00 sharp, and I will accompany you to Whitefield and see what I can find out from his staff. No promises, you understand, for I have no more influence on whom he will see than anyone else."

At 7:00 A.M. I picked him up in a chauffeured car. John and Aspi were also in tow. They did not want to miss the experience. We arrived at Whitefield by 8:00 A.M. It was a typical, small Indian town with dusty roads, barefoot and sandaled people walking along the roadsides, cars and trucks honking, and bicycles weaving between vehicles and people. Sai Baba's residence and ashram consisted of an enclave with very ornate entrance arches. His followers were beginning to gather under a large, gazebo-like structure. It was still early and not too hot. My guide instructed me to sit under the gazebo while he asked Sai Baba's attendants about the program of the day.

The agent returned ten minutes later and grabbed me, literally pulling me out of the gazebo. We ran to a long, low building with many windows on its sides. I was planted in front of the side door—not the main entrance—and told not to move. I was getting fidgety; the gazebo was filling up and I worried that I wouldn't be able to get a good seat. Ten minutes passed. Attendants came over to the building and opened the front doors. Then, from the inside, the side door opened. The agent pushed me in, immediately jammed me against the wall to my right, and told me to sit. As I sat cross-legged on the floor with my back against the wall, I noticed a chalk line three inches in front of my knees that ran the full length of the building. Another chalk line ran parallel to it, forming a pathway three feet wide. Aspi and John sat at my sides, and the agent sat facing me, directly across the path.

An extraordinary hush descended. The energy was high with anticipation. I sat quietly, my hands flat together in prayer style, with Vincent's and Finn's letters between them. I had decided not to write a letter of my own to Sai Baba. If he was truly an avatar, I thought, he would know psychically what my personal request was: clarity in my spiritual path and in my personal life.

"OOHHMM!!" The whole building vibrated with the universal sound. I joined with the other voices, repeating the sound, reverberating it through my nasal and sinus passages, and experiencing the depth of meaning and energy that can only exist at such a gathering. Sai Baba had entered the building and was standing on the podium. He looked exactly as I had seen him in my meditation. He stood smiling at the crowd with his arms stretched in front of him, palms up. He gently rotated them in an upward, semicircular motion as if he was weighing or feeling the energy in the building. He then stepped down from the podium and walked outside. I could tell he was walking along the side of the building where I was seated because people's heads turned and followed his motion past the windows. Then he reentered the building by the same side door I had come in. Now Sai Baba was standing ten feet from me. Everyone near him was trying to touch his robe or bare feet. Some were trying to give him flowers or messages. As he began to walk slowly down the aisle, people reached out to touch his feet. When he was abreast of me, he stopped, turned, and looked at me.

"Where are you from?" he asked.

"New York," I said.

Then, with that same familiar, knowing smile I had seen in my meditation, he said, "Welcome to India. I have been expecting you."

My mouth was paralyzed. He took my envelopes. The first one was Vincent's. He looked at it intently as if x-raying its contents. Without opening the envelope, he assimilated the information in a few seconds. The next envelope was Finn's. A smile of recognition crossed his face as he digested it. Then he looked at me again and said, "Thank you," and walked back up to the podium without stopping.

Sai Baba proceeded to lead the entire congregation in a Hindi chant with a haunting, sweet, melodious voice. The voice of love entered my soul. A speech followed, again in Hindi, with an English translation every few minutes. Not a word do I remember. However, I do carry with me the warm energy that I absorbed. We left the ashram around noon. The agent was beside himself. "I knew it," he said. "I knew you were a special person."

"Not me. I'm just a messenger," I said.

We all drove back to Bangalore stunned, our missions accomplished. John and I packed, thanked Aspi profusely, flew to Bombay, and the following day returned to New York.

When I got home, I called Vincent to report on my extraordinary trip. As luck had it, Finn was with him. In response to my report Vincent commented, "This was my sense of what your trip would be when I gave you my letter. Some of the letter's contents were personal, but I'll tell you what I asked for on behalf of humanity. I requested that Sai Baba intervene with the higher cosmic forces to find a cure for AIDS. Further, I asked him to send me a confirming symbol in the form of a white dove, if he should acquiesce to my request."

Finn cut in on the extension phone. "That's incredible," she said. "I made a similar request asking for a gold ring—for you, Vincent—in confirmation."

"Why a gold ring for me?" Vincent asked.

"You've been so active and have spent so many hours in hospitals helping AIDS patients, I felt you should receive recognition."

As we parted on the phone, with holiday wishes, all our hopes were high.

The next couple of days were joyfully hectic. I went Christmas shopping and welcomed all the children home from various parts of the country. Bette and I were now living without children at home after twenty-seven years of marriage. Many issues between us that had been swept under the carpet had surfaced. The kids' return for Christmas was a joyous relief. Eric, our oldest, finishing his master's degree in film, flew in from Los Angeles. Marc, in his last year at the University of Colorado, came in from Boulder. And Claire, our youngest, a sophomore at the University of Vermont, flew down from Burlington.

Our children, involved in their own worlds, were unaware of the tensions between Bette and me. Bette was as pretty as ever, with her sparkling blue eyes and auburn hair; what was lacking was the energy connection between us. She had a terrible fear of separation and loss, and her reaction to my Indian trip was no exception. Whenever I returned from traveling I was anxious to have sex with her—to express my love, my need, and our reconnection. I did not understand that she needed time to process my reappearance and let down her walls of isolation. I felt her coldness, and it was like a bucket of cold water on a hot fire. Steam rose but the coals fizzled. This Christmas, when the children came home within a few days of my return, they relieved all of Bette's fears in one fell swoop. Our holidays turned out to be warm and embracing, with the entire family in high spirits.

Three days before Christmas I got a call from Vincent. "Claude, you're not going to believe this!" he said.

"What happened?" I asked, more than mildly curious.

"If you recall, I always pictured in my mind's eye that the symbol for the AIDS foundation should be a purple rose. Well, two AIDS patients I had been working with in the hospital decided to give me a little present. It was a small box. When I opened it, there was a tiny white papier-mâché dove sitting on top of a purple rose."

I could hardly move. Tears were welling in my eyes.

"Claude, are you there?" Vincent asked.

"Yes, I feel Sai Baba's presence with us," I said.

"I do, too. Take care, my friend. Merry Christmas."

"You too, Vincent."

The blessings of Christmas were many, and the New Year rolled around. It was now 1988. Finn called to recount her wonderful time in Paris with her boyfriend over the New Year's holiday. They had stayed in a small hotel on the Left Bank and at the end of their stay retrieved their passports and jewelry from the Hotel's safe-deposit box. A plain gold ring was found, which belonged to neither of them. The hotel proprietress could not trace its origin, so she said, "Well, Madame, it's your lucky day. Have a good New Year."

Finn explained, "Claude, it was then that I realized this was the gold ring from Sai Baba for Vincent. I got back yesterday and immediately went to see him. It fit him like a glove. I'm so excited I can't stand it. God, I do hope this crisis comes to an end."

"It will, just as the plague did," I said.

"Claude, you sound so fatalistic."

"It's not for me to make a judgment. I was only the messenger. The message was accepted. Now it's all in God's hands. Goodnight, and God bless you, Finn."

Finn was a young, very dedicated helper and researcher for many AIDS projects. She took the AIDS crisis to heart with a matchless emotional intensity that carried over into her efforts to help all those in need. Few of us felt as deeply as Finn about human suffering. She always sought to relieve pain wherever she went. She died in 1989. I have missed her.

Vincent continued his untiring work for the cause of AIDS, but he himself contracted the disease and died in December 1994. I feel deeply saddened about his death, as Vincent was a special person in my life. He turned me to the path of spirit.

As for John Feuer, Aspi, and the others of the coffee world, I lost track of them when Bette and I moved to Santa Fe, New Mexico, in 1990. Because of this move, I resigned as chairman of the AIDS foundation. By that time, Finn was already gone, and Vincent no longer had the strength to continue.

Even though a saint like Sai Baba may agree to help a cause for mankind, this does not guarantee what will happen. The universe is more mysterious and uncontrollable than we like to think. As events in my own life were about to show, spirit often has plans for us beyond our wildest imaginings.

3 Chenrezi

Guides will come to you when you need them.
—Chenrezi

From 1987 to 1991, my experience with Sai Baba haunted me, and I turned my laser focus on learning every Taoist meditation available. I practiced one to three hours of meditation a day, traded commodities, and wrote a book about men's issues in the commodity world. I found my body's psychic and energy channels opening and clearing. The process, at times, involved great pain, because the energies literally had to burn through blockages in my body created by long-held emotional issues. Initially the energy moved through my mid-back. Then, over the years, it broke through the stresses held in my upper back and shoulders. My view of the world started to soften, but still I could never reproduce the experience I had in India with Sai Baba. During those four years I also studied the dharma as taught by the Drikung Kagyupa lineage of Tibetan Buddhism.

Centuries ago, Buddhism in Tibet took on many unique characteristics because of the work of Padmasambava, a great enlightened teacher who merged the native Bon religion of Tibet with Buddhism. He was able to bring together the best spiritual practices of both religions to create the energy-moving qualities of Tibetan Buddhism. The practices of Tibetan Buddhism felt somewhat familiar to me. I found I resonated more harmoniously with tantric meditation practices than with the technique of sitting in voidness that characterized Zen.

In the spring of 1987, Swami Sambavananda, at Marc's

ashram, invited His Holiness Kagbon Chetsong Rinpoche, head of the Drikung Kagyupa lineage of Tibetan Buddhism, to spend some time in retreat and give some empowerments, or initiations. The main translator and facilitator for his entourage was the Venerable Khenpo Konchog Gyaltsen Rinpoche, head of the lineage in the United States. Bette and I were in Boulder then, visiting Marc, and we were both introduced directly to Tibetan Buddhism and to Khenpo. We took refuge, meaning we became students and took protection in the Buddha, dharma, and sangha. *Dharma* means the teachings of the Buddha, and *sangha* is the community of followers. We were each given Buddhist names and did some further empowerments.

After one of the day-long teachings and meditations, the ashram prepared a meal for all the participants. After dinner everyone mingled and joked. The ashram members showed the monks various yoga positions, which then deteriorated into handstands and cartwheels. We all laughed hysterically watching several monks trying to hold their robes between their legs and do cartwheels. I saw how serious and present these monks were in their practice, and how equally present they were when they were having fun.

Two years passed before Bette and I met Khenpo again at Marc's ashram. This time he was alone and was giving a Phowa empowerment. The Phowa is a practice to prepare the individual for death. The practice is very similar to the Taoist advanced meditation of Khan and Li. Although this teaching should be obtained from a master, the basic technique is to shoot one's spirit from the heart through the main-body thrusting channels up through the crown at the time of death. In the Buddhist practice the energy movement stops at the crown, with the final thrust reserved for the day one dies. The Taoists, on the other hand, shoot the energy out the crown to experience the vibration and encounters of the astral world.

At the time Bette and I were doing these meditations our marriage was strained. I was moving out of my intense involvement in business and becoming more and more aware of our relationship. Participating in these spiritual experiences together was a salve on old festering issues between us that would eventually resurface. Bette was very moved by the various empowerments but would only practice the exercises at retreats or teachings with Khenpo. However, Tibetan Buddhism allowed me to have small openings in my meditations similar to my experience in India.

Almost four years after that turning point in India, I wrote an article about my Sai Baba experience. It was published in the January/February 1991 issue of *Body Mind Spirit* magazine. Among the many letters I received in response to the piece was one from a woman named Paulette Taibi. She wrote that her husband Doug channeled the revered Tibetan Buddhist entity of compassion, Chenrezi. Although I had heard a lot from Khenpo and other lamas about Chenrezi being the ultimate Buddha of compassion, I had not done a Chenrezi empowerment and meditation.

Chenrezi was an actual person who lived at the time of the Buddha and developed such love and compassion that he vowed he would emanate his energy to certain individuals until all sentient beings were enlightened. The Dalai Lama, head of all Tibetan lineages, is considered an emanation of Chenrezi. Most times Chenrezi is represented on *tankas* (paintings) as a completely white being, with four arms and one head, in a posture of compassion and wisdom. When the Tibetans refer to compassion they usually also refer to Manjushri and Vajrapani, beings who were not incarnated but who represent energy aspects of compassion. Manjushri represents the wisdom of the word cutting through illusion. Vajrapani represents the power of action in compassion. Without wisdom and action, compassion is meaningless.

With these images in mind, I listened to Paulette Taibi. She suggested we should meet. She and Doug lived in North Carolina while we lived in Santa Fe; however, we found common ground at the Sag Harbor, Long Island, seashore home Bette and I still owned.

It was August 1991, and I was alone in the Sag Harbor house. Bette had already left for Santa Fe, where she was studying for her master's degree in social work. The energy of our eventual separation was heavy in the air. Part of me already missed Bette's soft accepting ways, but other parts of me wanted her to be less reliant on me, to know deep in herself that she was complete and could fully live her own life. I had always required control in our relationship, most likely due to my own fears and insecurities. Whenever we were in disagreement, Bette would walk on eggs to avoid confronting the issue, even if I was wrong. As my spiritual consciousness evolved, I needed someone who would stand up to me. I had changed enormously over the past several years and needed an equal partner in our relationship.

To add to the tensions, Bette had yet to develop an interest in spirituality as deep as mine, although she had reluctantly learned the basic Taoist and Buddhist meditations to understand what I was experiencing. I felt that this gap between us was a deterrent to our communication and harmony. I did not understand that she experienced her spirituality through service and not, at that time, in the mystical meditations I practiced. I believed strongly that our relationship and marriage depended on her being able to love herself totally. In this respect she was a mirror for me. We both needed to love ourselves before we could share unconditionally with each other. But no matter the condition of my marriage, my quest for self-realization and spirit was motivated by a desire that could not be quenched. In this light, I was pleased to be by myself at Sag Harbor when it came time to meet a couple who over the coming years would turn out to be good friends.

Doug Taibi was a tall, thin, bespectacled man, well fitting the image of a professor. Paulette seemed his female twin, with brown hair and eyes and a similar gaunt appearance. She told me that Chenrezi referred to them both as Acea, representing twin flames, and indeed they were inseparable.

I had never met a channeler before. I had a few psychic friends and found that the things they said were, at times, entirely right; at other times, they were equally wrong. When wrong, they universally explained that we all incarnated with free will and that nothing was written in stone. Now a channeler was sitting in my living room and I was full of reservations. I asked Doug how he came to be a channel and what exactly that meant.

"I was dreaming one night," he told me, "and suddenly the dream became more real than reality. My father, who had died fourteen years before, was standing at the foot of my bed, smiling and saying he was pleased to see me. He told me he had a Tibetan monk friend he felt I should meet. Now mind you, my father was an Italian Catholic and had never had any interest in Buddhism or ever mentioned a Tibetan monk to me. Still standing at the foot of the bed, he told me his friend would call me in the near future. I was awakened from the dream by the ringing of the telephone. A Tibetan lama was calling, saying he was a friend of my father and that he would like to meet me."

Doug explained that he had always been interested in crystals and had already had the ability to see a person's aura, but had never been attracted to Buddhism. He was intrigued by the modest monk, and they became good friends. Over time the lama gave Doug teachings and eventually informed him that he, the monk, was Chenrezi, an incarnate but only for a brief period of time. He had come to work with certain people on Earth and Doug was one of them. Chenrezi said he would be leaving his physical form soon and the time had come for Doug's initiation.

For three weeks Doug prepared for his initiation with herbs and fasting. He was taught how to leave his body. At the end of the week a young monk joined them, and Chenrezi explained that the young monk would take care of their bodies while their spirits were gone. He would oil them with herbs and massage them so that all their organs would stay healthy, as they would be gone for several days. While he was out of his body, Doug traveled to

Tibet, visited certain sacred sites, and was initiated into complicated rituals, which he was not at liberty to divulge. When he got back into his body, he went on with his daily life.

About a month later, Doug received a call from the monk informing him that he was leaving the following Tuesday at 8:00 P.M. and that Doug should be ready thereafter to channel him. Doug and Paulette had a dinner date with some friends that Tuesday and decided to keep the engagement. During dinner Doug suddenly started to shake and break out in a sweat. Paulette looked at her watch and noticed it was exactly eight o'clock. They had to excuse themselves from the table, and Paulette drove home. A week later Doug started to channel Chenrezi.

"So tell me, Doug, why do you think this happened to you?" I asked.

"Chenrezi says the world is about to enter a massive change of consciousness, and that he will channel through me to help that process, and specifically to help Acea, meaning Paulette and me, in our evolutionary path."

"Well, I have never had an experience with a channel. If you are up to it, I'm ready."

"Yes, that's why I'm here—for you to meet Chenrezi. You have to understand that I'm a full-trance channel, meaning I leave my body and Chenrezi comes in, so I will have no recollection of your talk. It will be your decision if you want to discuss what transpired."

"I understand. Let's see what happens."

Doug took off his glasses and rings, sat quietly for a few minutes, and then appeared to undergo a transformation. Suddenly he opened his eyes, which seemed to sparkle a lot more brightly, and addressed me in a foreign but unidentifiable voice.

"Hello, I am glad we are finally meeting."

"Hello to you. Sounds like you have been planning to get us together."

"Yes, you might say that, although all events come in their proper time."

I had reservations that this entity sitting on my couch was truly the revered master of compassion of Tibetan Buddhist lore. I asked him many detailed questions about my past and was satisfied he had deep knowledge. I directed the rest of my questions to the realm of spirit, my main interest.

"I'm planning to go to northern India, Dehra Dun, to spend some time with the Drikung Khagyupa lineage of Tibetan Buddhism. Do you think that by spending a few weeks to a month there, I can improve my practice and path?"

"You need to go further north," he answered without hesitation.

"Further north? Any further north and I will be in Tibet!"

"Yes, that is what I mean."

I felt fear well up in my body. "The elevation is too high. I have a heart condition. I had a bypass in 1977 and an angioplasty two years ago. I doubt I could handle the elevation."

"Do not worry; you will be in good hands."

"What do you mean?"

"There are guardians where you need to go. They know what they are doing."

"What guardians, and where do I need to go?"

"Ancient spirit guardians as well as reincarnated beings. I will only say that the place you need to go is made in stone, not out of stone."

"That sounds like a cave. How do I find it? And at what elevation is it?"

"Guides will come to you when you need them. The elevation of the cave in your measurements is a long distance, over three of your miles."

"What! That's about 16,000 feet. My heart will never take it."

"As I said, you will be in good hands; it is your path to take."

"How do I find these guides you talk about? Would the Drikung lineage be of help?"

"Yes, that might be a good place to start."

I tried to probe him further but he refused to give me more specific answers. He indicated that he felt Doug needed to get back in his body because much time had elapsed. I thanked him for all the information, and he was gone. Doug came to in a daze. He said he felt his body had worked harder than usual. He was very hot.

Paulette came back to the room and gave Doug a loving hug. I invited them out to dinner and recounted my session with Chenrezi. The next day they returned to North Carolina. I had two weeks to ruminate before I returned to Santa Fe. My main spiritual path had been the Tao; yet for the last few years I had been more and more involved with Tibetan Buddhism. An urge kept building in me to return to Tibet—although I had never been there. The urge was to return to a life that seemed vaguely familiar. Now, suddenly, a channel claiming to be Chenrezi had instructed me to go to Tibet. I decided that if the forces of the universe wanted me to go to Tibet I would do so, heart problems or not.

At the time I was sponsoring a young Tibetan student at the Dehra Dun monastery school. He was the nephew of my teacher, Khenpo Gyaltsen. During my quiet time in Sag Harbor I made a decision to write to Khenpo about my extraordinary meeting and ask for his reaction.

4 The Venerable Khenpo Konchog Gyaltsen Rinpoche

I know where you need to go.
—Khenpo Gyaltsen

Two days after my return to Santa Fe, I received a call from Khenpo. He acknowledged receiving my letter and informed me he had a gift for me from his brother in India. "It's a small token of appreciation for sponsoring my nephew through the monastery school. I will be in Santa Fe on the last weekend of September to give some teachings at the *stupa*. Perhaps we could meet and I can give you the gift."

I thanked him for his brother's consideration, expressed my desire to see him, and invited him to stay with Bette and me. He accepted and agreed to stay on a few extra days so that we could meditate together.

Without ever acknowledging the possibility that the entity was Chenrezi, Khenpo went on to say that he found my experience with the channeler most interesting. As usual he was neutral, noncommittal, and simply accepted the story at face value. Khenpo was a human being who truly made no judgments and emanated compassion at all times. I had heard that he could be a tough taskmaster when students were lazy in their spiritual work. I had never seen that side of him but only sensed the man's inner spiritual strength. For me his patience, knowledge, and teachings were always available.

I met Khenpo at the Albuquerque airport. He had not changed in the two years since I had last seen him. I was always taken aback by the large size of his shaved head

The Venerable Khenpo walking Santa Fe basin.

compared to the rest of his five-foot-six body. He carried a large overnight bag on his covered shoulder, while his other shoulder was exposed, as is usual with Tibetan monks. His deep-orange/maroon robe stretched over his legs when he set out on his long-gaited walk. I scurried to match his pace. His brown face and sparkling black eyes beamed with a smile as we chatted our way toward my car. As we drove to Santa Fe he pulled out of his bag a beautiful, small, Tibetan sitting rug—a gift from his brother, which

I now sit on daily. I thanked him for his kindness.

Bette installed Khenpo in our downstairs guest bedroom where he could get up at 5:00 in the morning to chant and pray without waking us. For the next two days, Khenpo was busy giving teachings and empowerments at the stupa. Bette and I did not attend, since we had gone through this two years earlier.

My interpretation of empowerments is that they involve setting patterns within the body—patterns that affect the DNA structure. Because the patterns are complicated, they are presented in the form of visualizations that the student can assimilate. The empowerments convey great energy, which the apprentice must absorb to do the meditation effectively. The Drikung lineage emphasizes the tantric aspect of meditation, in contrast to the more mental orientation of other lineages. All lineages employ a great amount of chanting, which is important to set the right mood and vibration for a practice. Teachings, in contrast, are mainly intellectual in nature and give clarification to the empowerments.

In my own training, at times I found the teachings helpful. At other times I found them extraneous and simply concentrated on the meditation while the lama was speaking. To some extent I was frustrated by Tibetan Buddhism and what I considered the outside show versus the real internal energy work that I had yet to see being taught.

On Monday morning, after a hectic weekend, Khenpo and I meditated for an hour and a half and then had breakfast. I decided to confront my friend about my frustrations with Tibetan practices.

I told Khenpo how in the Taoist meditations we moved energy down the front part of the torso via the functional channel and then up the back of the torso via the governor channel to connect through the tongue. I described the more advanced meditations of clearing negative energy in the organs and opening the central thrusting routes, similar to the Phowa in the Tibetan practices. I asked Khenpo how these practices compared to what he was doing.

"Our practices are very similar," he said. "When we meditated together this morning, I had a feeling you were a high practitioner."

"Khenpo, I have a long way to go to be a high practitioner. Why don't you and other lamas teach your students the internal practices? Why keep them on the peripheral level?"

"So many people in the West are looking for a path but are not serious students. We test them by their perseverance, and then as they ask the questions, we reveal to them the inner work."

"Khenpo, I think you lose a lot of followers that way. The world is opening its consciousness; you must come forth with all your knowledge, both external and internal."

Much to my astonishment, he opened up fully and described in detail the internal energy work of the various empowerments and teachings I had done with him over the years. I got my notebook out and feverishly wrote down the formulas. We spent most of the day comparing practices and how they dovetailed together.

By midafternoon, we both needed a break, so we drove to the Santa Fe Ski Basin to walk and watch the sun set behind the Jemez Mountains. After five minutes of walking, we started to discuss my experience with Chenrezi and my possible journey to Tibet. I could tell from his tone of voice that he was now taking the information and experience more seriously.

That evening he led both Bette and me in a meditation that was much more meaningful to me with my new knowledge. Afterward, Khenpo kept us entertained at dinner with his unflagging sense of humor. I couldn't help but notice that Bette's eyes, even her auburn hair, seemed more alive as we talked and joked about various subjects.

Early the next morning Khenpo and I meditated again for two hours. We had breakfast, then did a walking tour of Santa Fe and stayed for lunch at the San Francisco Street Bar and Grill. The waiter came over to take our order. I ordered iced tea and a medium hamburger.

Khenpo looked at me with his big brown eyes, his brows raised, and asked, "Are the hamburgers good here?"

"Yes, some of the best in town."

He turned to the waiter. "All right, I will have the same."

I was always astonished when Tibetan Buddhists ate meat and at the same time tried to avoid killing any living thing. I myself had no problem with eating meat. Like the Native Americans, I believed in giving thanks to the spirit of the animal which gave its life so we could live. Both Khenpo and I bowed our heads in thanks when the hamburgers arrived. The air conditioning was on and I was concerned that Khenpo might be cold, with his thin robe and exposed shoulder.

"Khenpo, do you want my jacket? It feels chilly in here."

"No. Thank you. When we drove to town you asked me if I was too hot in the car, in which case you would put the air conditioning on. Do you remember?"

"Yes—I'm concerned for your comfort."

"That is not necessary. Westerners are too concerned with their comforts. They want to change the entire planet to fit their comforts instead of adjusting their bodies to the conditions of the planet."

That was all he said. The message was loud and clear. We should make the adjustments to accommodate Mother Earth.

Khenpo was leaving that evening for Albuquerque, where he was to give a teaching at a friend's home. Just before getting in the car, he held my arm and said, "When are you planning to go to Tibet?"

"Nothing is definite, but I was aiming for September and October 1992."

"All right. I know where you need to go. I will take you there. I will be your guide."

I was stunned. Just as Chenrezi had predicted, a member of the Drikung Khagyupa lineage would guide me. Suddenly the reality of the Tibet trip loomed large and real.

"That's fantastic, Khenpo. I'll take care of all travel and financial arrangements and keep you posted on the progress."

"That will be fine." His typical expression. Then he reached down in his bag and pulled out a *khata*, a white silk scarf, and put it around my neck.

"What is this for?"

"It is our tradition to give a khata when we recognize a high practitioner. I look forward to being your guide in Tibet."

I was overwhelmed with emotion and blurted out that he was the great practitioner and I only a lowly student.

"Do not underestimate your practices," he responded. "We will continue in Tibet."

5 Changes

Not such a tough guy after all.

After Khenpo left, I had much time to myself to reflect and explore not only my mind but my emotions. My commodities trading was coming to an end, although my computer was still hooked up to all the futures markets, particularly the currencies. I reluctantly concluded that trading was an addiction and that I was now involved more out of habit than joy. In fact, there was very little joy in my life at all. I moved through the day like a mechanical man. I was writing a book about my life in the international coffee world, but the work was constantly interrupted by phone calls to and from New York, phone calls about the markets to which I seemed to be chained.

Meanwhile Bette was deeply involved in school. Every morning she gave me a kiss and said, "Good-bye, hon. See you around tonight." She spent three days a week at the university and two days a week as an intern with an agency. We went out for dinner often, even though we both were good cooks and enjoyed the process. And although I was working on my book, I was unsure of myself. I was like a bear pacing in a cave.

On weekends I tried to initiate closer connections with Bette. One day I stood next to her desk chair and said, "Bette, let's cook up something for Saturday night—maybe invite some friends in?"

"I can't. I have to study," she said. "I have two papers due at the end of the month." She continued typing at her computer.

"For Christ's sake, you have a straight-A average. Take some time off for yourself."

She turned and looked up over her shoulder. "When you were studying for your MBA at night school and we had two children, I took care of everything. You do it."

I walked away in a huff, yelling back, "Bullshit. I give you all the time you want during the week. When I was getting my MBA I was working full-time. I think you're exaggerating your studies." But intuitively, I knew she was starting to build her independence.

Bette let out a deep sigh and moved her right hand in an erasing motion, "Okay," she said. "We'll cook together."

I could barely hear her from across the room. The tension was set for the weekend. We were like two strangers sharing the same house. I no longer felt joy in our relationship. My entire life had revolved around control: control of companies, control of situations, even control of my wife. I owned Bette like I owned the seashore house, the boat, my fast cars, in fact all the objects and people around me.

I abhorred the situation. My meditations had brought me deeply into my higher mind, where the cosmic reality that there was no such thing as possession became crystal clear. As I meditated more and more each day, I felt that all else around me was illusion. Yet even though I was prepared to let go of my possessions to the extent that they possessed me, I knew that making good on such a decision would take time. I possessed and was possessed by Bette. I could not break the vicious cycle that existed between us. I needed to let go, and she needed to discover who she was. We could not love each other on an equal basis unless we fully respected and loved ourselves.

On December 22, 1991, Bette and I would be married thirty-one years. I had been in and out of a funk for over six months trying to understand the emotional dichotomy of loving her and yet experiencing the joylessness of our relationship. This issue had been relegated to the back burner of my mind while I had been running around the world making deals. However, the need to work on our relationship had come to a boil now that I had retired from my business. As I divested myself of possessions and spent more and more time on my spiritual practices, I was actually becoming more controlling and possessive where Bette was concerned. I wanted her to grow, to become independent, to be self-assured, to be her total being, all of which I felt I had clearly defined. I wanted her to change, but on my terms. Needless to say, this would never work.

Our children were aware of the tension but regarded my domination and Bette's submissiveness as a familiar drama. Claire, our youngest, had come to live with us after graduating from college; she saw the difficulties firsthand and chose to ignore them. She was a pretty, twenty-four-year-old blond with other agendas. Eric, thirty, was busy with his film career in Los Angeles. Marc, at twenty-seven, was busy creating a family in Colorado.

I wanted space. I needed to be alone. I longed for a new life, to see with new eyes. I knew I needed to change but didn't know how. After my heart attack, I had spent five invaluable years in therapy switching my focus away from business and toward spirituality. This time I did not want therapy. I felt that the changes I needed had to come from inside me, from spirit, not from a manipulation of my mind.

In the fall, Santa Fe enjoys beautiful sunny days with bright blue skies and much cooler nights that foretell the onset of winter. I started on a program of hiking at least three times a week for three to four hours at a time to condition myself for Tibet. One morning in early November, Bette asked to join me on my hike.

"Sure, I'd love the company."

We each took a fanny pack with water, first aid kit, and some munchies and set off. We climbed steadily at around nine thousand feet in the Santa Fe National Forest, ten minutes from our home. Sunlight filtered through the ponderosa pines. Bette interrupted the silence. "Claude, I feel you so distant. What's going on?"

The simple sentence struck as deeply as a rattler hitting its mark. My deep self knew that movement was necessary and I had to speak my truth. I was formal and stiff as I tried to explain.

"Bette, I think we need to separate so we can both find ourselves. I can't live this way. I feel you're walking on eggs when you are around me, and what I want is you, not some person in fear of breaking a delicate tie that exists between us. I need to move out of the house, find my own place, and then perhaps our dialogue can be on an equal footing."

"Is this decision final?" she asked.

Suddenly, at that very moment, my mind was made up and I told her so.

Tears filled Bette's blue-gray eyes and ran down her cheeks. I felt so sad, so ashamed to be the cause of such pain. My heart was wrenched, for I loved her deeply, yet I knew we could no longer live together if we were ever to find ourselves and our individual inner joys. I went to hold her tenderly, to assuage my own guilt and shame. She pulled away and walked down the mountain. I followed silently a hundred paces behind, and we drove home without a word. A week later I moved out of the house and into a rented apartment.

The news came as a bombshell to our children. Claire's blue eyes initially flooded with anger; then she continued with her life as if nothing had happened. I would take her out to lunch to keep in touch and talk.

One day Claire gave me her big smile and then lectured me. "Dad. You always want Mom to be and do what you want. She needs to lead her life the way *she* sees it, not your way."

I leaned into the table. "Listen, that's why I left," I said. "She can find herself, and I need to do the same."

She laughed, flinging her long, blonde hair back over her shoulders. "I swear the two of you are like kids—you enjoy sex together but then each of you has a tantrum in your own style."

I was taken aback. "Claire, what's this sex stuff?"

She laughed again, tilting her head back as if to make fun of me. "I asked Mom if sex was good with you. I figured if you didn't have good sex, the marriage would not work. But since you do, I'm sure you guys will work it out."

Then the waiter came over, and the conversation moved on to her daily life.

From time to time Claire would lecture Bette on feminism and independence, but she continued to believe that one day we would get back together.

Our middle child, Marc, became the gentle supporter of both parents. He called me weekly to see how I was doing.

"Howdy, Dad, what are you up to?" he asked one week. I could hear his smile over the phone and sense his compassion.

"I'm fine, got the apartment settled and feel at home. Look forward to your coming down from Boulder and visiting."

I could hear his hesitation. He explained he did not want to hurt Bette by visiting me. Besides, his wife, Anne, was now three months' pregnant, so she and Marc were not traveling. I understood but felt a certain loneliness, a need for physical family companionship. I hid my feelings and said, "You're right. How is my wonderful daughter-in-law doing with my grandchild in there?"

I could hear Marc exhale relief. "She's doing fine, and the doctor says our baby girl looks good too."

Eric, the oldest, was having the most difficulty dealing with the separation. He saw me as an antagonist. He supported Bette by phone as best he could and gave me short shrift. I was deeply hurt. I felt I had lost a child, as he would barely communicate with me when I called, and I always had to initiate the contact.

One night we had a hurtful conversation. "Eric, how are you doing?" I asked.

"I'm okay," he said.

I could tell from his tone that his head was fixed, his temples pulsating, and his dark brown eyes flashing anger at the sound of my voice. I wanted to connect but did not know how. As softly as I could I said, "You sound a bit tense. Any problems with work?"

He shot back, "No. Look, I talk to Mom on a regular basis, and she's hurting. I try and support her and give her comfort. You're a big guy; you walked out. You can take care of yourself—you don't need my support."

I was stunned. I hung up. I broke down and cried for two hours. I felt very alone and sensed a welling fear about my physical well-being. I no longer had anybody to take care of me in the event of a bad cold or a medical emergency or hospitalization. I felt vulnerable—not such a tough guy after all. It was a difficult realization for me to accept. But the real test of my vulnerability was still to come.

6 Torax

The energy spins so fast that the
structure glows like a star.
—Michael Winn

A few weeks after Bette and I separated, I flew to New York to see my sister, who was about to turn fifty. The weather was cold and crisp, and the sun cut between the tall buildings; it was my favorite time to visit the Big Apple. I reconnected with old friends, including Juan Li, a senior Taoist teacher who had just returned from three months of teaching in Europe. Juan was a tall, lanky man, half Chinese and half Puerto Rican, with soft brown eyes and long, frizzy hair worn rolled up in a bun. I always felt comfortable in his company, and our time together usually revolved around mystical and metaphysical talks. He had lived in Nepal for six years, where he had learned tanka art, and he now illustrated Taoist and other spiritual books.

Juan had visited Tibet less than six months before and brought me up to date on conditions there. He recommended various herbs and Chinese formulas for my trip. We walked through Chinatown, visited his favorite Chinese pharmacy, and picked up the various herbal formulas. We then went over to Soho, south of Houston Street, to have lunch. I asked him what he was up to.

Leaning back in his chair, Juan explained he was going to Egypt to paint and then hook up with a group planning some sort of initiation in the Great Pyramid. The group would be led by Michael Morgan, a Taoist and a student of Master Mantak Chia. Perhaps we had met at one of the retreats?

I was intrigued. "No, but the name sounds familiar. What makes this trip special?"

"Michael channels an entity by the name of Yokar who was an Atlantean priest and scientist. I've never heard him, but he's a good friend of Michael Winn, who talked me into joining since I was going to Egypt anyway."

"Mike Winn? Really?" Mike was another Taoist senior teacher. I had heard a lot about him, but we had never met.

Juan continued, "Well, he only lives a few blocks from here. Why don't we drop in? Winn can give you more information about Michael Morgan, Yokar, and the trip. I think he's helping Morgan with a book."

"Sounds great," I said.

Winn lived in a brick building on Thompson Street painted a bilious green, with an Ethiopian restaurant on the ground floor. Juan and I walked through the restaurant. I noticed that all the food was served and consumed without utensils, African style. The clientele spoke in French, Swahili, and African tongues, interspersed with bits and pieces of English. Juan knew the cook and one of the waiters; they spoke in French, as they were from the Cameroons—strange for an Ethiopian restaurant. I smiled and said a few words in French. I was well acquainted with the Cameroons from my coffee wheeling-and-dealing days.

By now my curiosity was piqued. I wanted to know a man who owned such a building and ran an Ethiopian restaurant in Soho. We took the back stairs up to Winn's apartment on the second floor. Half a dozen shoes were lined up in front of the door, and the smell of Chinese herbs filled the corridor. Juan and I took off our shoes and knocked.

The door was opened by a blue-eyed, red-headed man. Winn was about five foot eight and had a full red beard. His speech was clipped and staccato. After comparing stories about Master Chia's teachings, we asked about the details of the Egyptian trip. Winn explained that if I joined, half the group of twenty would be Taoist. We would be initiated by Yokar and, at worst, would have some great meditations together while visiting the majesty of Egypt.

"What are these initiations about, Mike?"

With an air of mystery and enthusiasm, he admitted that he did not exactly know, except that he had many sessions with Yokar and long talks with Michael Morgan. The best he could piece together was that Yokar was going to reactivate the vibrations of various temples to initiate us. Egypt had been an outpost of Atlantis when the latter blew up, so the high priesthood of Egypt had actually been taught and initiated by the Atlanteans. Winn went on, "Yokar, through Morgan, will only state before the trip that whoever gets initiated will be working for the Most High for the highest good of Planet Earth."

I sensed a magnetic pull to join the group. "I'll be in Thailand two weeks before, to do a meditation retreat with Master Chia as a review—I want to be certified to teach the deeper practices," I said. "Since I'm going to be in that part of the world, I might go back to India to explore and maybe see Sai Baba again. I could then come to Egypt."

Winn interjected, "If you think all the meditations and alchemical formulas taught by Master Chia are powerful, wait until you learn some of Yokar's stuff."

"What do you mean?"

"The Taoist practices for the most part are yin, or water oriented, although they are meant to bring out the yang, or fire component, by their alchemical, transformative formulas. Yokar's energy teachings are pure fire, meant to accelerate the change of vibration in your DNA structure and bring you closer to the frequency of spirit."

I was really intrigued. "Can you give me an example?"

Winn was eager to relay his knowledge. "The practice or alchemical formula is called the Torax, and I've been practicing it for a while. But each individual has a different reaction to it. So I suggest you review it with Yokar if you meet him."

I was leaning forward on the edge of his couch, anxiously awaiting the details. He took out a piece of paper and drew a three-dimensional pyramid with a four-sided base, creating a five-sided figure like the Great Pyramid of Giza in Egypt. At each corner of the four-sided base of the pyramid he drew a small tetrahedron, a pyramid with a three-sided base. So there were a total of four tetrahedrons dangling from the corners of the larger pyramid. He looked up from his drawing and said, "Now this is important. There is another pyramid that I will draw shortly, but this lower one must get going first."

I had no idea what he was talking about. "What do you mean, 'get going first'?"

"You're used to doing difficult visualizations from your Taoist work and tantric Buddhist meditations; well, this one is the toughest." He continued, "First you picture a clear crystalline pyramid with similar tetrahedrons hanging from its base. You visualize this inside your body and look down on the top of the big pyramid. The point on top is at your solar plexus and the base with its four tetrahedrons runs across your sexual organs, at the level of the tip of your coccyx. You visualize this crystalline structure in your lower torso. Then you get yourself aroused, without a partner, and as your sexual energy manifests itself you start rotating the pyramid, clockwise for a man and counterclockwise for a woman. The more you arouse yourself, the faster the pyramid should spin as you look down on it internally. As you are aroused you draw your sexual energy into the tetrahedrons; do not have an orgasm. You pull up your sexual energy internally in the same fashion taught by Master Chia in his book *Taoist Secrets of Love*."

I responded, "Yes, I know, but you're not pulling the sexual energy up your spine like the Tao, you're putting it into the tetrahedrons. Then what?"

Winn was enthusiastic, as he knew I could visualize the procedure. "Okay, so the tetrahedrons are heavy with your sexual energy, and they are being pulled out by centrifugal force due to the spinning of the large pyramid. The greater your arousal the faster the spin, and the greater the outward force on the tetrahedrons; eventually the energy spins so fast that the structure glows like a star. Now here comes the difficult part. With your will centered at your solar plexus you pull the tetrahedrons in and up. When you have the whole procedure going you will hear a definite sound internally." He said I would feel very hot and possibly see color changes in the crystalline structure of the pyramid.

Winn started to draw again on the paper and continued, "Once you feel you can do this consistently, then you internally construct the exact same pyramid and tetrahedrons, but inverted, in your upper torso. That is, the point of the upper pyramid is again at your solar plexus, but it goes up and forms a base through your heart center with the tetrahedrons at the corners. You start to rotate this pyramid counterclockwise, clockwise for women. You fully get in touch with an emotion, whatever it may be—love, anger, compassion, or so on. The emotion does not matter as long as you are fully engaged with the feeling. You draw that emotion into the upper tetrahedrons and again they'll fly outward because of the centrifugal force. The more you're in touch with the emotion, the faster the spin and the greater the outward force. This time you center your inner will at your sexual center, drawing the emotion through your solar plexus. You pull in as well as draw down the emotional energy. Again you will hear a sound, subtly different from the first. Possibly you will see color changes. The pyramid will glow. You will have to try the exercise to fully understand the dynamics."

Winn said that to him the inner imagery appeared as DNA. It was like spinning cones of energy in an apparent elliptical form. "Over time," he told me, "this practice will refine your vibration closer to the subtle body vibrations. The higher the vibrations, the closer you get to the Most High, as Yokar would say."

He stopped and looked at me intently for a reaction. I nodded my head in affirmation. It sounded like a powerful practice with some of the characteristics of the Taoist fusion

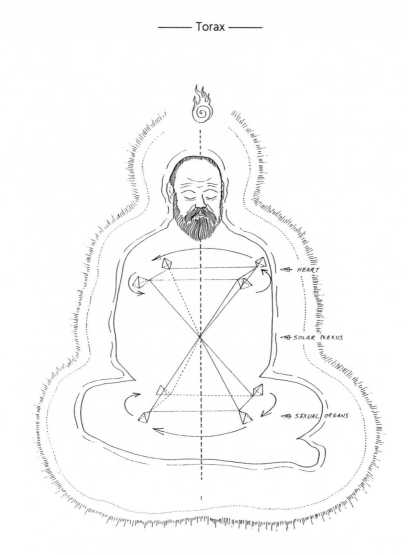

Torax, courtesy of Michael Morgan, Channeler of Yokar.
Copyright © Michael Morgan, 1995

of the five elements. If so, the sexual energy, the energy of creation, was being used to transform emotions. I commented, "What is curious is that the solar plexus is used as the center for alchemical transformation."

"You have to understand that this is the beginning practice. There are higher forms of Torax, which Yokar will not teach until he is satisfied that the individual's vibrations have been refined for the next change. I do not know the higher practices, but I suspect their center is the heart. If you think about the practice it makes sense to first soften or change the vibration of the center of power, the solar plexus."

After listening to Winn I decided I wanted to go to Egypt, meet Michael Morgan, and become a student of Yokar. I was convinced Yokar would provide the next steps in my spiritual growth. Over the past twelve years I had completed and used all of the Taoist teachings that Master Chia had given me, and I felt it was now time to move to a higher octave.

I left New York, and two weeks later I sent my check to Michael Morgan. I was anxious to accelerate my growth, so I practiced the Torax as often as time allowed before the trip. I found the Torax more difficult than the basic Taoist sexual recirculation methods. The difficulty I found was that, besides retaining my sexual energy, I had to visualize the big pyramid and the four tetrahedrons, get the structure spinning, and then pull my sexual energy into the tetrahedrons. The exercise required that I master my internal will and tension at the same time that I relax enough to keep the whole picture together. I found I would lose one part or another if I got too tense about succeeding.

Once I was able to really accomplish the spinning at great revolutions and pull the energy up, then indeed the crystal pyramid glowed. Indeed, as Winn had said, the lower pyramid was the more difficult to master. The second, inverted pyramid on top seemed to gain its own momentum from the lower one's energy. The whole process was very difficult to hold while in a state of sexual arousal, and I continually had to rearouse myself to keep feeding energy to this incredibly ecstatic encounter. Along with the glow of the counter-spinning structure came high-pitched sounds. But I sensed something missing. I would learn more later.

The "big draw" Taoist practice of pulling up sexual energy before orgasm with a partner to send it to other parts of the body is very helpful. However, I would recommend that the beginner first learn the microcosmic orbit, as described in *Awaken Healing Energy through the Tao* by Master Mantak Chia. This can be followed by practices in his books *Taoist Secrets of Love* for men and *Healing Love through the Tao* for women. The Torax can be mastered without the Taoist methods, but I suspect it would take greater determination and a longer time to achieve.

I spent the New Year's holiday of 1991 at my son Marc's ashram above Nederland in Colorado. Two days of chants and meditation and a wonderful reconnection with Swami Sambavananda prepared me for my upcoming journey.

7 Thailand/India

*A very old man in tattered clothes
came up to the window.*

From Santa Fe, the easiest route to Thailand was via
the West Coast and a connection through Singapore. I had
not been in the city-state of Singapore since 1980 and
found it not much changed in twelve years. However, it
was vastly different than my first visit in 1969. Singapore
was still big business, but now it was oriented toward
electronics, banking, and paper trading rather than toward
the bulk cargo and coolie labor that I had known. My
one-day layover allowed me to adjust to the humidity, heat,
and Eastern mentality. I loafed, walked around the busy
streets, poked into the various shops, and gorged myself
on great Chinese cooking and a hard-shell crab dinner.

My mind was flooded with memories of my free-wheel-
ing days in the back alleys and the old *saipan* inner harbor,
where I had done business with some of the cleverest
traders of the world. I felt I was back in the hands of a
familiar mistress, exotic in her perfume, calling to me once
again to do a deal. The old feelings rushed through me,
yet my head was clear. Business was behind me; I was on
a spiritual journey. I reflected that the intensity I had
brought to the business world was now manifesting itself
in my spiritual quest.

The next morning I flew to Bangkok. The airport was
teeming with people, but customs and baggage handling
moved efficiently. As luck would have it, an American
couple going in the same direction agreed to let me ride

along in their hired van, and three hours later I was deposited in front of Master Mantak Chia's condo in Pataya. I was looking forward to spending some time with Chia and reconnecting with old friends.

I was astonished by the amount of construction and the number of high-rise buildings right on the beautiful sand beaches, Miami-style. Palm trees hung limp in the humid atmosphere and I could see mirage-like islands shimmering in the distance of the South Sea. It was late on Sunday afternoon, and the heat was starting to abate. I took the elevator up to Master and Maneewan Chia's penthouse apartment on the fifteenth floor of the building. I knocked on the door and Maneewan opened it, her smiling five feet of femininity enveloping me. We spoke awhile and then she assigned me to my room, which turned out to be a sparsely furnished apartment: bedroom with bed, living room with plastic couch, private bath, kitchenette, and one air conditioner that barely kept the temperature down. I was pleased to be alone—others were crammed three to four to an apartment. At 6:00 dinner was served in the common dining room. Master Chia came in and invited me to join him at his table.

"Claude, good to see you here. I would like you to help teach Tai Chi and Iron Shirt early in the morning. You are the only teacher here this week. Next week others are coming, so they will relieve you."

I enjoyed him. He always came right to the point when he wanted something. Being a teacher meant being on the beach at 7:00 A.M. to teach the exercises. This was followed by Master Chia leading meditation at 8:00 A.M., then breakfast. Later, there was class, then lunch and break, then classes again until 5:30 P.M. The week was uneventful. The second week brought more and different students for the advanced classes. I knew many of the people; several were there, as I was, to review the courses and prepare for certification as advanced teachers. One of my good friends, Kathy Corbo, and her boyfriend Gerald were present. Gerald was a world-class martial artist from Bermuda who took over the morning Tai Chi and Iron Shirt instruction. Gerry Gelb, another friend, also arrived.

Kathy was a blue-eyed, dark-haired woman of Italian descent, five foot two and packed full of energy and mischief. Her full lips easily parted into a smile, revealing white, evenly spaced teeth. Gerry Gelb, a computer consultant with Bell Labs, had blue eyes, curly blond hair, and a large beaked nose.

Up to this point I had remained secluded, except for classes, teaching and studying for my upcoming tests. Now I started going out at night with Kathy, Gerry, and Gerald. Pataya had been a rest and recreation area for American troops during the Vietnam conflict. The current attractions included kick boxing and sex and transvestite shows—quite a contrast with the spiritual work we were doing all day. Since many of our practices dealt with transforming sexual drive into higher forms of energy, viewing Pataya's baser instincts was amusing to say the least. After three nights we had our fill and settled into the condo lounge for review, philosophy, and general catch-up on each other's news. I brought them up to date on my plans. Kathy's blue eyes opened wide when I spoke of my upcoming trip to Egypt.

"My God, Claude, I visited a psychic friend of mine about a month ago and she predicted I would be going on an important spiritual journey to Egypt. I dismissed the idea as absurd. Tell me more—maybe I should join you. I can work like crazy when I'm back in Boston, then come to Egypt."

Kathy worked as a nurse in the intensive care unit of a hospital associated with Harvard. She worked the weekend night shifts that paid time-and-a-half so she could have the rest of the week off. I told her what I knew about the trip, Michael Morgan, and Yokar. Kathy remembered Michael from her early work with Master Chia, many years before. She gave me her big, full-lipped smile. "I'm going, that's it. I need to be there. I'm joining you."

"Kat, don't get your hopes up. The trip might be full."

"I know I am supposed to be there—there will be room." And that was that.

Gerry Gelb listened, relaxed and smiling as we talked, but when I got onto the subject of my upcoming trip to Tibet in the fall, his body language changed. He became alert and listened closely to the tale of Chenrezi and my connection with Khenpo. Just as suddenly as Kathy had decided to join me in Egypt, Gerry committed to traveling with me to Tibet. The prospects of my upcoming trips were gathering energy.

The rest of the week went smoothly, including my testing. As usual, Master Chia tested me personally with intricate and detailed questions. The rule was that any three teachers could test an applicant, but Chia always insisted on reviewing my knowledge himself. The other teachers kidded that I would never pass Tai Chi (which I have not), even though I always help teach it at retreats, because Master Chia wanted perfection from me. I passed all my other tests and decided Tai Chi would never be my martial art. Goal accomplished, it was time to move on to India.

I landed in Madras expecting throngs of porters to overwhelm me. Nothing. Only a few of them asked politely if they could carry my bag and find me a taxi. On past visits to India I had always feared being smothered by crowds of beggars searching for work or handouts. This time, my attitude was one of compliance, of compassion. My pocket was full of two-rupee notes, and I intended to distribute them without hassle, without trying to avoid the poverty and squalor that thrust itself in my face. Yet no one bothered this weary traveler. I was journeying alone. Although I was in one of the densest population centers on Earth, I felt alone. I had left details of the trip to providence, making advance reservations only for the first two days in Madras and the last three days in Bangalore and Bombay.

I checked into one of the better hotels, showered, and enjoyed the comforts of luxury. My path had given me success in the material world. I felt that whatever had brought me to India did not require a journey of discomfort and deprivation. My financial well-being was meant to be used wisely for self-growth and service to humanity.

The next two days were spent visiting Madras. Nothing sparked my interest. I needed to get out of the city and visit the temples and sacred sites of southern India; to become more introspective and at the same time totally open and receptive to my surroundings. I was marking time between my Thailand certification and the Egyptian initiations. I lounged around the hotel pool and thought of Bette. I missed her presence, her familiarity. Or perhaps I just missed the presence of a woman companion or being in touch with my own feminine, receptive side. I kept recircling my sexual energy into my brain; but throughout this journey my reflections kept coming back to my need for companionship, my yearning to integrate personal relationships into my spiritual work.

I hired a car and driver. I was not going to drive on the left side of the road in the cacophony of Indian traffic, and I decided that my experience in India did not need to include public transportation. The driver's English was passable, when absolutely needed, but not good enough to carry on a conversation. Perfect. I wanted to be alone amidst all the noise, honking, dirt, and heat of the open road. The car was not air conditioned, and we traveled with all the windows open. The car seats were plastic; with the heat and dust, I was covered with a fine, sticky film within an hour.

The narrow roads were crowded with fast-moving cars, buses, and lorries. Each time my driver pulled out to pass, I found myself staring straight at a huge oncoming lorry or bus; at the last minute he would pull back into our lane. I was tempted to tell him that I was not in a rush and he could go slower. I thought better of the idea and said nothing. I feared the reprimand would affect his judgment, and then indeed we would have a fatal collision. I started reciting mantras. My body was tense. Then I thought to myself, "This is ridiculous. If I'm going to die or be maimed on an Indian road, so be it. Let go—flow with the universe!" The tension flowed out of me. I stopped reciting mantras. I became one with the heat, dust, smells, noise, and the plastic seat of the car.

The driver wanted to start early each day, around 5:00 in the morning, to avoid the midday heat. Initially I acquiesced, but then realized his desire was not in accord with my body rhythm. After the second day we started between 8:30 and 9:00 A.M. I was in a "I don't give a shit" mood and wanted to blend with my surroundings. I wanted to smell the earth, sewers, and vegetation. I wanted to feel the heat and taste the dirt—I wanted to be part of India. We drove south from temple to temple, and small town to small town. The further south we moved, the greater the heat and the more intense the greenery. Farms and vegetation were more abundant, and there was less poverty. As we moved south each temple blended into the next. Statues and shrines of Shiva, Ganesh, and Brahma, darkened by centuries of dirt, were indistinguishable from each another. I was bored and was marking time.

As the car bounced, so did my thoughts. Was this really a journey to find my inner truth, or was I running away from myself? I felt aimless. I thought about how I used to try to control every situation around me. I recalled Christmas holidays that I wanted to be so perfect—according to my definition—that no one could be spontaneous, and so emotions flared, culminating in tears. In letting go of my control, I was encountering the joy of surprises in my life's journey. I was learning that each thing, good or bad, had a purpose and required full engagement of the moment's energy—including my present boredom.

We finally reached Madurai, the site of one of the largest Shiva temples in India. I gave the driver a nice mid-journey tip, making him feel a lot better about the discomfort of our schedule. I had planned two days in Madurai but decided I could visit Shiva's temple thoroughly in one day since my psychic channels were not picking up anything of interest.

I kept checking myself. Was I open to any experience that came along? The temples I had visited were dark and dingy with *ghee*, or melted clarified butter. Following custom I walked barefoot through the dirt from shrine to shrine. The temple was the same as all the other temples except bigger, with more shrines and statues. Beggars waited at the entrance gates and for the most part did not hassle me, continuing the pattern of the entire trip. I wondered whether my long ponytail made them think I was a true pilgrim and not a tourist. The few beggars who did ask for alms on my journey seemed to have a different aura, and I willingly gave them a few rupees, or, if a child, a ballpoint pen.

We left Madurai early Thursday morning and headed north along India's east coast. In the late afternoon we stopped at Pondicherry and I checked into Sri Aurobindo's ashram hotel. My room overlooked the Bay of Bengal, with the waves pounding on the beach. The room was clean and extremely basic: no towels, soap, or toilet paper were provided. There was a mosquito-net contraption for the bed. The beach was only a hundred yards away and promised a swarm of night visitors. I inquired of a surly woman at the front desk about the ashram schedule. In a haughty "I'm doing you a favor" tone, she informed me about breakfast and dinner hours and about a meditation in the garden of the main building that evening. I reflected that religious or spiritual devotees of any sort often think they are better than others. I let the annoyance go and walked over to the meditation.

There was no moon and the sky was pitch black, but the garden twinkled with hundreds of lighted candles carried by practitioners. I found an open space by a fountain, put my day pack down to sit on, and crossed my legs. I straightened my back and placed my hands in the meditative position. I cleared and opened my meditation channels and immediately became aware of strong energies all around me. This was the first time on this trip that I felt a strong spiritual presence. I connected to the ephemeral. The next thing I knew, the meditation was over.

The next morning I found my driver covered with mosquito welts as a result of sleeping in the car. Except for night pests, Pondicherry was a clean, well-laid-out town. It still retained the flavor of its former French influence, which included the *kepi* worn by the local police. We drove off to Tiruvannamalai and the temple that held Ramana Maharishi's shrine. I knew there would be great energy from Maharishi's ashes if he was the enlightened being that he was reported to be.

In India, as in Tibet, when a great evolved being dies, his ashes are put in a shrine. The custom in Tibetan Buddhism is to look for a solid piece of matter, a "pearl," that has not burned to ash. This pearl carries the energy of that person and is implanted in a *stupa* where devotees of the dharma can come to practice and be in touch with the essence of that great being. I hoped I would be able to connect to Maharishi's energy and thereby further connect to the higher vibrations of spirit. We arrived in the dead heat of noon. I took off my shoes and started walking around the large temple complex from one shrine and altar to another.

A young Hindi priest came up to me and asked in broken English if I wanted to go to Maharishi's shrine. Yes, indeed I did. He brought me to a dingy stairway leading down into dark catacombs. The space was damp, and smelled of earth and must. The second my feet hit the last step I was overwhelmed by energy, as if a heat wave emanated from Maharishi's shrine. His ashes were buried within. I thanked the priest, made a donation, and sat in meditation off to one corner in the dark. I could clearly feel and visualize waves of golden particles radiating from the shrine. Once accustomed to the energy flow, I drifted off into other dimensions. I became aware of feet shuffling by me—an hour and a half elapsed. I did not want to leave this wonderful feeling, yet knew that whatever I needed had been received and no further attachment was required.

The next day I changed my plane tickets and headed for Bangalore, where I checked into the Sheraton. I hung out for a day not wanting to trek immediately to Sai Baba's ashram in Puttaparti, a three-hour drive each way. That day I stayed in my room, watched television, and reflected on my loneliness. As a great Zen teacher might say, "What's wrong with loneliness?" I realized that going through these massive changes required my total commitment to spirit. I wrote a letter to my executive assistant asking her to cancel all my trading subscriptions and to close down my computer connections to all markets. A weight lifted from my shoulders. I was now prepared to reconnect to Sai Baba, knowing that my first experience would never be replicated. Sai Baba was known to be able to materialize gold rings and other objects for his devotees. He was also reported to be able to be in two places at the same time as well as to take several forms, to "shape-shift," as Native Americans call it. So when I made arrangements the next day for a car and driver, I was prepared for any experience.

I found out that Sai Baba gave *darshan*, a passing of energy or blessing, at 2:30 P.M. I had ample time to leave Bangalore at nine, arrive in Puttaparti around noon, have lunch, and then go to darshan. The driver was well acquainted with the road and we made good time. The further we moved from Bangalore, the scantier the vegetation became. The countryside turned brown, sunbaked, parched, and almost desertlike. There was absolutely nothing between Bangalore and Puttaparti except for a few small villages eking out a living from the hardened soil. I had decided not to stay in one of the bare rooms of the ashram, opting instead for the discomfort of the return journey and the comfort of good food and lodging at night. Halfway to the ashram, the driver pulled over at a roadside stand and asked me, "Would you like some tea?"

"No thanks, I'll just sit here and drink my water." I never went anywhere in hot countries without a large bottle of water. The driver went off to get his hot tea, half filled with milk, at the stand, and I sat sweltering on the hot plastic car seat. A beggar came by and I gave him a few rupees. The driver got back in the car and we were off. At 12:30 P.M. we arrived in Puttaparti, and I asked the driver to join me for lunch in a tiny restaurant he recommended. Afterward he showed me around the enormous ashram. Sai Baba had established schools from first grade through college level, as well as one of India's largest and most modern hospitals. An airport was under construction, and within a year flights would be arriving full of avid followers.

I went to the darshan gathering area where lines were forming and numbers assigned to prioritize the seating arrangements. An hour went by. Then our group of several hundred men was let in on one side of an outdoor seating area while a similar group of women was let in on the other side. Another half hour passed before Sai Baba came out in his familiar orange robe and Afro hair style. I was seated in one of the rear rows and got only a distant glimpse of him. He went around touching people for half an hour and left. After another three-hour drive I arrived back in Bangalore. I informed the driver we would do the same thing the following day.

The next morning at 9:00 we were on the road again. The heat of the day was building when again the driver pulled over by a road stand.

Same conversation. "Would you like some tea?"

"No, thank you, I'll just sit here and drink some water." I was sweating profusely, merging with the plastic seat, feeling hot and disappointed that nothing had come of yesterday's trip. A little girl came by the open car window and handed me a garland of flowers with one hand while she held the other out for a donation. I gave her some rupees and put the garland around my neck, feeling more at peace, in a total reverie. A very old man in tattered clothes came up to the window. His face was extremely wrinkled, with white stubbles for a beard and grayish-white disheveled hair. He half smiled at me, exposing two lone yellow teeth, and extended his hand into the cab. I thought to myself, "Here we go again," and gave him a few rupees. He did not go away but started mumbling a chant. I wondered what he wanted. He joined his hands in prayer as a sign of respect, bowing his upper torso but fixing his eyes on me. This was most unusual, so I put my hands together as well and bowed to him in respect.

As I looked up, our eyes connected. There was an explosion. Energy poured out of his eyes into mine and unconditional love overwhelmed me; the sensation was the same that I had experienced several years back in the Bombay hotel. I was in ecstasy, with tears pouring down my face. As the realization came to me that I was in Sai Baba's presence, the driver came back to the car and we moved off. The beggar disappeared. I sat silent and stunned. I wanted to turn back but knew he would be gone.

I continued on the journey knowing that I had completed my experience in India. I had been tested, and I knew nothing would happen at the ashram. Events transpired as foreseen. I spent the next two days alone, meditating in my room; then I flew to Bombay and connected to my Cairo flight.

8 Egypt

Your father has laid out a banquet
waiting for your return.
—Yokar

I arrived in Cairo a day ahead of Yokar's group. The local tour representative whisked me through all the debarkation formalities, then drove me to the Movenpick Hotel in Giza, right across from the Great Pyramid. The next day I wandered through Cairo's bustling traffic, with its throngs of people, small shops, and little cafes. Both the locals and tourists were drinking Turkish coffees.

People in Egypt said the weather was hot, but for me it felt cool compared to India. During my walk through the *souk* (central marketplace), I reflected on how I had signed up for this trip on blind faith. I had read several books on Atlantis, none of which had resonated with me. Yet I was convinced that Atlantis had existed and that parts of this lost civilization still remained below the Atlantic Ocean, causing strange phenomena such as those that occurred in the Bermuda triangle. Moreover, this was the first trip I had ever taken as part of an organized group. Previously, I had always made my own arrangements. I was following my deep intuition. Whatever awaited me had to be important.

The group arrived around 4:30 P.M., and I was introduced to Michael Morgan. He was a heavyset man, taller than average, but his presence made him even larger than his true physical dimensions. His blond hair was threaded with auburn, and his hazel eyes were kind. He smiled easily, even though he was harried from checking the entire group into the Movenpick Hotel.

Egyptian Hieroglyph

I met the others over an early dinner. My Taoist friends were there: Kathy Corbo, Michael Winn and his wife Joyce, Juan Li and his girlfriend Renu, Gunther, and Rylin. The group included people from all walks of life, including a registered nurse, a bicycle messenger, an accountant, house-wives, businessmen, a commercial video producer, spiritual teachers, and me, a retired commodities trader. The youngest, at twenty-six, was Alain, the bicycle messenger. Gunther and I were fifty-four. I found it interesting that there were twelve men out of a group of twenty-two; in most spiritual gatherings I had attended women generally far outnumbered the men. We came mainly from the United States. The group included two African-Americans and a Chinese-Cuban, my friend Juan Li, whose girlfriend, Renu, was originally from Germany. I wondered what energy had brought such a potpourri of people together in Egypt.

After dinner we all gathered in the conference room to have our first session with Yokar. Before going into trance, Michael Morgan asked us to introduce ourselves and briefly tell how we had come to join the trip. It quickly became apparent that all of us were on spiritual or shamanistic paths of one sort or another. We were all proud of our commitment and listened attentively to the others' stories. A dark-haired, dark-eyed man with a large nose and swarthy coloring stood up. "I'm John Paccione," he said. "I have no idea what I'm doing here. Each one of you is in touch with spirituality. I came because of my accountant, Duky, here." He pointed to a short, bald man with sparkling mischievous eyes. "He told me about the trip and I thought it would be a gas to come—so I did. Can you tell me, Michael, why am I here?"

Michael Morgan smiled an easy smile. "Ask Yokar when I'm in trance," he said. And the introduction moved to the next person.

Rylin was a tall, thin woman with dark auburn hair, deep-set eyes, and elongated features. "Gunther and I have been Taoists for many years, and when we heard that Michael was leading a tour with so many friends present, we had an urge to join. We were not in a financial position to handle this trip, and then suddenly, at the last minute, a small stock we owned tripled in price due to a takeover. We made just enough money to come. The other factor is that I have breast cancer, and I feel this trip is important in my evolution at this time." Gunther, a dark, curly-headed, wiry man, sat next to her with tears flowing down his cheeks.

Each person had a different reason for coming. No commonality ran through the group. John Paccione had come out of curiosity, Rylin because of cancer. Kathy believed she would find another spiritual guide. Mike Winn and Joyce had come because of their belief in Yokar. Others had felt connected to ancient Egypt, some had sensed a calling, and I had come because of the other Taoists and because I thought I could deepen my commitment to spirit.

Michael Morgan announced that he was going into trance and that Yokar would come in. He requested the lights be shut off. Their electromagnetic fields disturbed Yokar. Someone lit candles around the long conference table, and the lights went out. Michael sat quietly, his eyes closed, in an apparently meditative posture. Suddenly his entire body collapsed in the chair. Then he began to twitch, and he gave out a few snorts as Yokar manifested. Yokar then sat erect on the hard chair, his eyes closed, both feet apart in a rigid pose. This posture was very different from Chenrezi's fluid movement and open eyes.

"Good evening," he said. "I am Yokar. How can I be of service?"

His voice was deep and authoritative. It projected no nonsense. Diane Morgan, Michael's wife, acted as moderator. Diane was a pretty, blue-eyed blonde with a soft, accepting way. She started out, "Yokar, we are all present and we are wondering what common thread binds this group together for the upcoming initiations."

Yokar responded, "You are all here because you have been chosen. Let me be more specific. I come from a stellar mind, an ascended master, who is with the Most High. A call has gone out to many. You have been chosen because in your free will you have responded to that call from the Most High. As most of you know, I once was an Atlantean on your Earth as a priest and scientist. Atlantis blew up because our people fell in love with technology and lost their connection to spirituality, to the Most High. Your civilization finds itself in the same predicament.

"The Most High has therefore ordained that the Earth must be saved," Yokar continued. "It must be rejuvenated from its present condition. To do so, the Earth's energy grids—or ley lines, as you call them—must be changed. These energy grids represent its nervous system. All the old power sites will soon disappear, including the Great Pyramid. I do not necessarily mean that they will be physically destroyed, but rather that the energy current beneath these sites will be relocated to new sites. For example, three ley lines cross under the Great Pyramid. These lines will dissolve, and new ones will form elsewhere. To accomplish this, the Earth will go through great physical changes. You will see earthquakes in places never seen before. Great storms and winds of up to two-hundred, even three-hundred miles an hour, will occur. Fire storms will develop, volcanoes will erupt, and continents will go through massive changes.

"The Earth has been weakened by man's follies and therefore does not have the energy to accomplish these necessary changes by itself," Yokar said. "The Earth needs cosmic energy of a particular vibration beamed down to energize the new lines. Contrary to what most of you believe, power comes from the cooperation of all energies in the universe. Compare the Earth to one of your great corporate leaders who, without the cooperation of capital and labor within the company, has no power alone except as a single person. The same may be said about your political leaders—without the cooperation of the body politic, there is no power. And so to effect these necessary changes in the Earth, you have been chosen to cooperate with the Most High.

"I will put you through initiations at various sites along the Nile, culminating with the Great Pyramid. These initiations will open your various chakra centers, which will then be sealed shut with particular resonances in the King's Chamber of the Great Pyramid. This will accomplish a change in your DNA, which will attune itself with the higher vibrations of the Cosmic World. In brief, you will become antennae for the energies to be beamed down. More training and information will be forthcoming after you have all completed your initiations."

I was stunned. Never in my wildest dreams had I imagined this was the purpose of the trip. Yokar asked if there were any questions. Someone asked, "Yokar, can you tell us when these Earth changes will occur?"

"From my position there is no linear time. Therefore it is difficult to be accurate for you. The only statement I can make is to tell you the changes have already started. I must mention that along with the physical changes of the Earth there will also be political and financial changes. The world's economic system as you know it will suffer a complete collapse. Look around you, read your papers.

Massive changes have already occurred, such as in the Eastern Bloc, and will continue. When all is complete, the Earth will be a marvelous planet to live on. You will once again learn to cooperate instead of compete."

"Yokar, where should we live to be safe?" asked someone else.

"Each one of you will be where you need to be when the time comes," he said.

"Yokar, how and when are we going to be antennae for the energies of the Most High?" asked another.

"Further instructions will be given after your initiations. You will need three to six months to assimilate the patterns that will be implanted into your cell structures. Relax. We will monitor you, and all that is needed will be provided in its appropriate time."

"Yokar, if changes have already started to occur, why does the Most High need us as antennae?" came another question.

"Because the changes so far are minor. Once you have all assimilated the pattern, you will be coordinated to beam the energy into the new grid system. I repeat: All in the universe functions on a system of cooperation. The Most High needs your cooperation as well as that of the Earth elementals, whom you will be taught to contact, to effect these changes. I will elucidate more over the next six months. Any other questions? If not, I must let Michael come back into his body as it is heating up."

"One more question, Yokar" said John Paccione. "What am *I* doing here? I'm not spiritual. I was brought up Catholic, but I don't go to church and don't follow the religion."

"The fact that you are here means your higher self heard the call. The main reason the Most High called you is that you know how to yield to its will. You know what I am referring to."

John's head bowed and nodded in acquiescence.

There were no more questions, and Michael came back in. He explained that his body was "overheated." Yokar beamed energy to the participants in the session after scanning them for the amount they could handle. The more he beamed, the hotter Michael's body got.

As the hour was late, the meeting broke up. I turned to Kathy and said, "I can't believe that the Most High needs us to help change the Earth."

Kathy's blue eyes looked tired. "Let's talk about this tomorrow. I'm going to bed."

Jeff Glick, my assigned roommate, was walking with us. He said, "I think Yokar meant help in a broad sense. Not necessarily on the physical plane, but energetically and spiritually, as people will be panicked as these changes occur. My perception is that on this trip we will become more attuned vibrationally and therefore more able to help others."

"Interesting view," I responded, "but I'm skeptical about the whole scenario."

Over the next few days I found that others shared Jeff's perception. As for me, I was waiting to be shown, to be convinced.

Jeff, a tall, thin, young man from Boulder, Colorado, was pleasant to room with; he did not snore, but he put up with my own trumpeting. Over the next two days we visited local tourist attractions and coalesced as a group. Assigned to us was Amr, an Egyptologist who imparted classical interpretations of the antiquities in the Cairo Museum and elsewhere along the trip. I enjoyed the dichotomy between the official "civilized" interpretations of the ancient sites and Yokar's explanations. According to Yokar, the original pyramid and temples were built as outposts of Atlantis and eventually were copied by Egyptians after Atlantis disappeared.

The Nile was considered by the Atlanteans to be equivalent to the human spinal cord. Through it, great energy could flow, as it did in the spine during mystical and tantric practices. When I looked at a map of Egypt, I saw that the Nile did in fact resemble the human spinal cord, ending in the delta at Port Said, which resembled a brain. The Atlanteans, Yokar said, built the original temples along power points of the Nile that corresponded to the human chakras. Each temple was imbued with its chakra's corresponding vibrational energy. This energy would be used to awaken, and heighten, the consciousness of the initiatory candidates. These initiations would proceed from south to north, culminating in the Great Pyramid at Giza.

In ancient Egypt, Yokar explained, human egos came to believe over time that *they* were essence instead of the Most High. The priesthood became more elaborate; it embraced the dark side of the occult for power and lost its understanding of initiation. Similarly, the pharaohs' lust for power and luxury overshadowed their connection to spirit and their role as protectors and benefactors for the people. As the true meaning and purpose of the temples disappeared, new temples with greater opulence were built on old sacred sites. In some cases, when old temples were destroyed, new ones were built incorporating some of the old stones. Such were the teachings we received from Yokar as he set out with us to reverse this process.

On our second day in Cairo, a group of us had lunch together at a small outdoor grill. We were telling stories of our past. I asked John Paccione to tell me what Yokar had meant by his comment "You know how to yield to the Most High."

John gave one of his big toothy grins. "There are several instances, but I'll only tell you one story as the typical example of my journey." He said that about a year before, he had been working in his office in Manhattan and decided to go for a lunch stroll. On his way back to the office he noticed a sun lamp for sale. He bought it and carried it up to his office. At the end of the day he had one more customer to call. He decided to turn the lamp on and get a tan while he was on the phone. He had not read any of the instructions and simply turned the lamp on, staring into it during his conversation with his customer. The call lasted longer than expected—forty-five minutes. Finally, John hung up the phone and turned off the lamp.

"I was dazzled, my eyes were seeing specks, and my

vision was unclear and blurry. I figured I had looked into the lamp for too long and my eyes needed to adjust. I left my building and headed for my carpark, two blocks away. By the time I was halfway down the block, I could see nothing. I groped my way back to the lobby of my building. My eyes were wide open, but all that came through was pitch black. I went up the elevator, counting the buttons from memory, and then felt my way to the office. I managed to get the key in the keyhole, opened the door, found my desk chair, and sat down. I just sat there, blinded for life.

"I thought about it. I was nearly fifty and I decided I'd probably seen enough. I thanked God for all the splendors I had seen." He then called his sister, explained what had happened, and asked for a ride home. She and his brother-in-law nursed John's eyes with compresses and drops for two weeks before his sight came back.

I now understood. John did know how to yield to the Most High. Letting the will of the Most High flow through me was a lesson I still needed to work on. I knew I would be tested.

Next day, the group flew south and boarded the *Nile Beauty*, one of the larger Nile boats. The cabin Jeff and I shared was comfortable, although noisy at night. It was under the dance floor.

The first evening, Michael and Yokar held a session for the group in the boat's dining room. Michael told us that he had completed a similar tour with thirty Japanese people two weeks before, and each member of the group had experienced unusual physical and emotional releases at various stages of the initiations. He warned us to be prepared but said he did not want to discuss the subject until our own trip was complete.

After these comments, Michael left his body and Yokar came in. We were told that all our first chakras were already open, otherwise we would not be able to operate on the Earth plane. Our first initiation would take place the following morning at the temple of Kom Ombo in the Holy of Holies chamber, where our second chakras would

*Michael collapsing as Yokar leaves his body. Amr,
our Egyptologist, in the foreground.*

be fully opened. Yokar instructed us to get out of our
heads and into our bodies to fully incorporate the experience, especially afterward, so the initiation would take
hold.

Each initiation would involve a specific vibration. Yokar

would clear the sacred area, call in the temple spirit guides, and then "Vrill" us. Vrill was a subvocal language. First, Yokar would picture the energy mentally; subsequently the vibrations would flow through his mouth from a spot halfway between his heart and throat centers. The practice would be a transmission of sound, pitch, color, feeling, and pattern. There were seventy-two letters in Vrill, corresponding to the seventy-two names of God in the old scriptures. Every Vrill transmission would have a subtle energy communication. The novice could best help the initiation take hold, particularly the patterning of the DNA structure, by staying away from analysis and use of the mind. The Vrill would work in any event, but the process would be accelerated when not interfered with by the human ego-mind.

The next morning we headed to the Kom Ombo temple. The new temple had incorporated in its structure certain seed stones from the older temple, which empowered the new building with the particular energy, or vibration, needed for its initiatory purpose. Yokar had instructed Michael where these stones were located, and not all were in the Holy of Holies chamber as theorized by the classical archaeologists. Once the stones were located, Michael went into trance, and Yokar came in to pronounce the sacred words and initiate each of us individually. I found the experience of Michael in trance and Yokar using the Atlantean language interesting but still had questions about the reality of the entire situation. My mind was analyzing the experience, and I wondered whether indeed I was being guided by supernatural forces in my journey.

After the initiation at Kom Ombo, we returned to the *Nile Beauty* for our journey north toward Karnak and Luxor for our next initiation. The Nile was wide and flowed slowly. The waters were filled with debris ranging from plastic bags to dead donkeys. The sun beat down hard. The weather was dry and at least twenty degrees hotter than in Cairo. But the boat's motion provided a cool breeze as we moved among great sand dunes, small farming plots, and villages clinging to the river banks. I felt as if I were in a dream, simply a pair of eyeballs floating between the sand lines and the reality of the inhabitants.

Suddenly, at 4:00 in the afternoon, I lost control. I was sitting on a deck chair next to Kathy and I started giggling uncontrollably. She cocked her head to one side. "Claude, what's so funny?" she asked.

"I don't know. I can't control my laugh. My head feels strange, as if things are moving around in it." By then I was laughing hysterically. Kathy got caught up in the laughter, then others around me did too. Everyone was laughing. Between giggling fits Kathy blurted, "What is going on with you?"

"Kat, I can't control it," I said. "It feels like the old days when I smoked grass."

My laughing spasm continued even as we moved into the dining room for dinner. I sat between Michael Morgan and Kathy. I addressed Michael. "My head really feels strange, as if my brain is being reoriented. I can't control my laugh."

"Perhaps the boys are rewiring you," he said.

"What do you mean?"

"As I said at the beginning of the trip, strange things will happen to each of you. There will be a cleansing so that higher vibrations can operate within and through you. In your case, as you are very mental, it's possible your head is being short-circuited."

Kathy, who was a psychic, cut in. "Yes, that's it. Your head is being rewired; that's the confirmation I'm getting through my guides."

"Great," I said, and once again burst into hysterical laughter. It was very catching. The entire dining room was now laughing, including two other tour groups traveling on the boat. My condition persisted until 1:00 A.M. with my poor roommate Jeff laughing with me, unable to sleep. Finally I collapsed and slept until 9:00 A.M.

During our next two initiations, I was much more present, and used my senses without interpreting or judging. I felt that indeed my brain had been rewired. I was much more attuned to my inner body and spirit. I could feel waves of subtle energies coursing through me. I was losing my doubts.

There was some free time one afternoon so I decided to have a private session with Yokar. In the cabin, Michael went into trance and Yokar came in, saying, "Greetings to you and blessings from the Most High."

"Greetings to you, Yokar," I replied. "This is the second time I have met with a channel, and I have many questions about this journey and other matters."

"We are here to serve. What can I answer?"

I was always intrigued by his "we" and "I"; nevertheless, I got right into my questions.

"What happened to me last night with all the laughing?"

"Michael pretty much answered your question," Yokar said. "We had to rewire your head to be receptive to all the vibrations and changes we are inputting."

"That brings me to the question—why *me*?"

"You have a question about your worthiness. Do not. You would not have been called if you were not worthy. You know the story of the prodigal son?" I nodded. "Well, you are as he—you are lost, wandering, while your father has laid out a banquet waiting for your return. Continue on your path, for you shall be reunited with him."

I felt my heart center open and a warm energy enter. Tears welled in my eyes. Yokar commented, "You know your initiation earlier this afternoon at Luxor was related to your heart center."

"Yes. Thank you, Yokar."

"You are welcome."

I sat quiet for a few moments before my next question, absorbing the energy emanating from Yokar.

"I have been told by another channeler that I should take a trip to Tibet. Could you comment on that?"

"Moment, please." Yokar seemed to be having an internal conversation or to be reading other realms. Then he came back. "Yes, I see you have a contract you must fulfill."

"What do you mean?" I asked.

"Well, it appears that you will shake hands with death, and it is not clear whether you will come back."

I thought about my heart attack and the bypass operation to my lower anterior descending artery I had gone through in 1977, as well as the angioplasty I'd had in 1989. I felt as if an ice pick had been driven through my left shoulder blade, the location of that artery. I was in excruciating pain. I asked, "What do you mean 'shake hands with death'? And what contract?"

"You struck a bargain many centuries ago, and you must now fulfill it. In that process you will shake death's hand."

"What bargain? Did I bump somebody off and now need to make amends?"

"No, quite the contrary. You saved someone's life and they owe you a life."

"Wait a minute. I don't need to go to Tibet and face death with the idea that somebody there will try and save my life. No problem—they're off the hook! The bargain is canceled. They don't owe me anything."

"You don't understand. You will receive a great gift."

"I don't get it," I said. "I have to face death to get a great gift? No thank you. I will pass."

"You have put off for many centuries fulfilling your bargain. We believe this time you are ready. The gift you will receive is beyond your human comprehension."

"So what is this great gift?"

"If I told you, you would no longer perceive it as a gift. You must prepare for the journey. It will be hard and hazardous."

"Yokar, what you're telling me doesn't give me much encouragement. Why should I do this?"

"Because you are a warrior, and you like to hone your sword to its finest edge."

"Yokar, I am not a warrior. I have never been in the military."

"You got that type of warrior out of your system when you were a Goth. You were involved in the sacking of

Rome. You bathed in blood and finished the experience in one lifetime. Since then you have been a different warrior—many times in the military, but always as a builder, advisor, or strategist. You were a gazer in Atlantis, meaning an astrologer, a counselor to the body politic. That is still your nature. You have been a warrior in the business world and quite successful. It is now time for you to use what you have learned to be a peaceful warrior—a warrior of the spirit."

"I have a sense that I should be teaching Taoist meditation and other spiritual practices."

"Yes, that is exactly what I am referring to. You must teach and counsel your old friends on Wall Street."

"Yokar, I haven't kept in touch with any of them." I explained that I felt I needed to publish *Strong Brew*, my book about the international commodity world, before I could teach.

"You need not have it published to teach. Teaching comes in different forms. Your friends will seek you out as the Earth changes start to occur."

"Are you saying I won't get my book published?" I asked.

"It will be published, but perhaps not in the sequence you think. If you come back from Tibet, you will write other books. Very few things are ordained from the Most High, so I cannot say for sure any outcome. You have a free will, and that free will determines the outcomes."

"One more question, Yokar. Can you tell if I'm doing the Torax properly?"

Yokar explained, "You are rushing. This practice will change your vibration. Your being and your consciousness will accelerate. To fully develop your inner changes you must be sure each step is fully activated."

I needed specifics. "I thought I was doing each step fully. I'm getting the sound of a high-pitched turbine when both pyramids are going full speed and I see or sense a glow."

His response was direct and emphatic. "You are not developing the lower pyramid properly. You must be

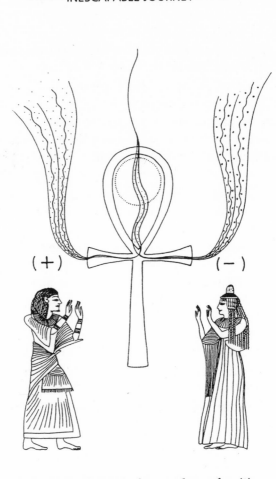

*The life force is a Triune force made up of positive
and negative and the neutral force.*

excited to the point of wanting to enter a woman. Then
redirect the energy into the fast-spinning tetrahedrons. The
structure is spinning so fast you nearly lose control of the
centrifugal tetrahedrons. With your inner will, not your
brain will, but your deep inner-core will from your heart,
you pull the energy in and up toward your solar plexus.
The pyramid will have a tremendous glow, and the sound
will be deeper and different from how you describe it. You
will know it when you hear it. What you are accomplishing

here is the accentuation of the neutral force, the resultant of the life force of the universe."

I wanted to know more. "What do you mean, 'the resultant of the life force'?"

"The life force," he said, "is a triune force made up of the positive-propulsive, which is yang or male; the negative-attractive, which is yin or female; and the neutral force, which is the resultant of both. This is symbolized by the ankh of Egypt: the two opposing forces blend in the void, the oval, to create the neutral force. Your civilization does not yet understand the power of the neutral force. All your motors and machines deal only with positive and negative energy to propel them. The real power is the neutral force. So by activating the lower pyramid you are creating neutral force. Your sexual energy in the centrifugal tetrahedrons is the positive-propulsive, and your inner will pulling in and up from your heart through your solar plexus is the negative-attractive. The glow and sound that ensue are the neutral force, which can be used to power everything. When you are fully powered, start the inverted pyramid as you have been doing. You will then get a second sound, and the two together will form a chord. That vibrational sound is unique to you and is your signature as you travel through the universe."

I was elated. "This makes more sense. Will I be able to hear that sound internally when I'm not doing the Torax?"

"Yes, of course. Once you become proficient you will be able to create the neutral force at will, and this will change your entire being. Then you will hear your own sound in the background, much as you hear your car's engine as you drive but pay it no mind. I feel Michael's body heating up, so I should leave pretty soon."

"I would like to continue our session tomorrow," I said. "I need to understand more about the implications of Tibet."

"We will take it up tomorrow," Yokar said. "Until then I extend to you the blessings of the Most High." Yokar then extended his right hand, his palm facing me, and his fingers slightly curled. His hand moved up and down and somewhat sideways in a way that was similar to the Sign of the Cross but different. He pronounced several Atlantean sounds, with Vrill, and I felt a peaceful energy bathe my body.

"Thank you, Yokar," I said. And he was gone.

Michael struggled to get back in his body, then looked at me in a daze.

"You guys must have had some session. I'm really cooking."

"It was a humdinger. He told me I was going to shake hands with death."

At dinner that night the subject of how Michael had become a channel came up. Michael explained that he had been in a fatal car accident—at least it was fatal as far as he was concerned. He believed he died, and he recollected having a meeting with the Most High whereby he agreed to come back to Earth to work for the One. Michael said his brain had been so severely bruised that the neurologist told him it would take a year before he would regain the full functions of his mind.

Diane then explained that she took Michael to a hands-on healer friend who let her medical guides work on him. During the second session the healer stopped and told Michael she was seeing a ten-foot-tall spirit next to him who wanted to communicate through her. That spirit was Yokar, and he asked permission to rewire Michael. Michael acquiesced, and three months later he was fully healed. Shortly thereafter, he started to channel Yokar. His story confirmed what Chenrezi had told me about full channelers of ascended masters.

After dinner I took Rylin aside and asked her about her cancer and how she was dealing with the prospect of death. Rylin explained that she had accepted the concept of death if that was what was to be; her difficulty was with the method by which she would come to her death. I felt anxious as she spoke, and my compassion went out to this tall, bright woman. The cramping in my left shoulder blade at the mere suggestion of my journey paled in comparison to her present state. She had not accepted the idea that she might not be able to heal herself, nor could she accept being maimed. As she spoke I realized that death in Tibet in itself did not hold great fear for me; rather, what frightened me was the idea of being maimed physically, emotionally, or otherwise. The specter of pain, vulnerability, and reliance on others to take care of me was overwhelming. The fear of loss of control over my body and destiny loomed large in my mind. Each time I thought about having a heart attack at seventeen-thousand feet, with no help in sight, I felt the familiar ice-pick jab in my left shoulder blade. I decided that in my next session with Yokar, my being maimed would be the central topic.

The next day Michael Morgan and I met again in my cabin. He went into trance, and soon Yokar was with me.

"Greetings to you," he said.

"And to you, Yokar. You've set my wheels in motion."

"Sounds like you have decided to go?"

"Yes. You know me, I don't back away from challenges, particularly if they include fear. I just need to define and understand the process, particularly as it could concern my being maimed, physically and emotionally."

"Very well, we can start the process now."

"Yes, by all means," I agreed.

"Picture yourself at sixteen thousand feet in Tibet. You are climbing with some friends and your guide. As you climb you become aware that your feet are getting heavy. The climb is becoming more difficult, and you find you need to rest. Your guide motions you on, as there is a long distance to go. You push on, and now even though the air is cold, you feel sweaty. Your feet and legs get heavier, and you start to wonder whether the perspiration you feel is actually mugginess, a different sensation from that of just physical exertion. For you know very well what this means."

And indeed I did, as the vivid memory of my heart attack and the clammy heaviness in my body came back to me. I again experienced the ice pick being jammed in my left shoulder blade. Yokar continued, "You are determined to go on, and so you keep climbing. Now a heaviness—even a pain—develops in your chest, particularly under your arms, and this pain travels up into the armpits and undersides of your arms. Your sensation is a clear symptom, and your mind is struggling not to panic.

"You are stopping more frequently now, more than every five minutes. The guide motions you to keep up. You are really struggling, and the pain reaches you in the throat under your chin. You are stopping every five steps, and the guide, impatient, is motioning that you must keep moving. You get up and start to climb again, and suddenly there is an explosion in your chest and a rushing sensation to your head. Your legs collapse. Your companions stand around you and give you water to drink but you know that is of no help. Your mind is now in a panic, and your thinking is vague and fuzzy.

"Through a haze you hear your friends discuss what to do with you. A change of plans is necessary. You have to be carried down the mountain. This, my friend, is what you need to process to go to Tibet. You must learn to yield to the will of the Most High and let the life force flow through you. You have much preparation and work to do, for as I have told you, the journey will be difficult and hazardous. I promise you that you will be pushed beyond your limits."

"Yokar, this is a tall order," I protested. "I have a tremendous pain through my left shoulder blade into my heart."

"Yes, I know. This pain is a blockage of the life force. You must learn to let it flow through you. Your preparation will require your yielding, your flowing, your opening to the life force in all aspects of your being."

"How do I do this?" I asked.

"You have already started, my friend. Your preparation for this journey began even before we met. You must now accelerate your opening, as your time is short."

"I guess we've covered the subject," I said. I realized

Author, in foreground, sightseeing with group.

the rest was now up to me. "Yesterday you suggested that I might be writing more than one book and that I might be teaching in the future. Doesn't that imply I will be returning from Tibet?"

"What I have told you is only a possibility. Whether or not you come back will depend on your preparation and the lessons you learn. You have free will, my friend, and you will determine how the life force flows through you."

"Well, if I come back from Tibet a cripple, will I have the energy to accomplish what I feel is my destiny—writing and teaching?"

"The Most High only has equal partners," he said. "You will have enough energy to accomplish what you have come to do."

Again, from Yokar, I had the overwhelming sensation of unconditional love encompassing me. My eyes filled with tears. "Thank you, Yokar," I said.

"You are welcome, my friend. Until we meet again, I send you the blessings of the Most High."

By late afternoon everyone in our group, excluding me and one other person, had come down with dysentery. The problem was traced back to the rice at lunch, which had been prepared with unfiltered water. I had eaten the rice, but it had not affected me. Someone asked Yokar at a question-and-answer session after dinner what was going on.

"There is a general cleansing occurring for those who need it for the next initiations," he said. Yokar wanted each person to be rid of any poisons or foods in the body that might affect the flow of vibrational energy during the remaining initiations. These initiations would involve the upper triangle of the throat, third eye, and crown chakras, which demanded the free movement of the subtler vibrations. The diarrhea varied from mild to disastrous during the two-day cleansing. People took various Chinese herbs, Western medicines, and homeopathic remedies to quell the onslaught. When it was all over, I felt the group was more conscious and attuned to the initiations.

After this incident our trip went well. We completed our initiations along the Nile and took in many tourist sites with our Egyptologist, Amr. Once back in Giza, all that was left was the work in the Great Pyramid, which included opening the crown chakra and the final sealing of all the chakras. I felt this would be similar to the sealing of the five senses, referred to in the Taoist canons but not, to my knowledge, taught by anyone. Michael had made arrangements with the Egyptian authorities to use the pyramid at night and thus avoid the crowds.

We fasted for thirty-six hours, starting the night before the final day of initiation in the Great Pyramid of Giza. Then we entered the pyramid at exactly sundown. The transition from the golden light of the desert to the dark, heavy stones of the pyramid was a jolt. Michael left the group to climb up to the King's Chamber and channel in Yokar. After all the guards left, their chief shut off the lights. We were plunged into darkness. Mike Winn and Diane Morgan turned on flashlights so we could don our

My knees and thighs hurt from crouching as I moved up the corridor.

specially marked robes. Diane then anointed each of us for the initiation. The flashlights were turned off.

In single file we slowly made our way to the corridor leading up to the King's Chamber by feeling our way along the wall. The corridor, or tunnel, was at a thirty-degree incline with only three-and-a-half feet of head room. I was located at about the halfway point in the queue.

Even though Michael had described in detail the entrails of the pyramid, encountering obstacles in the pitch black was a shock. The reason the corridor was built this way, according to Yokar, was to force the neophyte to prostrate himself on the way to the chamber of ultimate initiation, the King's Chamber. Yokar had explained that the pyramid

The high priest would sit on the uncarved boulder next to the sarcophagus to initiate the neophyte inside.

was never a tomb, and that the sarcophagus we would encounter in the King's Chamber was only used for initiations. The high priest would sit on the uncarved boulder next to the sarcophagus to initiate the neophyte inside. Yokar told us he would reactivate the chamber and perform once again the rites he had done so many times in Atlantis, over ten thousand years ago.

My knees and thighs hurt from crouching as I moved up the corridor. Then suddenly I became aware of music floating down from above—the sound of deep drums and flutelike instruments along with certain rattle sounds. As the group moved higher, the sounds became much louder and set up vibration waves along the walls. I entered the

Yokar in priest Horus' garments, as visualized by Juan Li.
Drawing by Juan Li.

chamber and was able to stand up. I heard Yokar incanting strange words, which bounced off the walls. I felt very alone in a huge, cavernous space and had the feeling there was no ceiling. Were my eyes seeing stars, the velvety sky? Could the top of the pyramid be open? I had to reassure myself of my sanity by extending my hand slowly in front of me until I could feel the person next in line.

Suddenly the music stopped, and all was silent in the total blackness. Only the small beam of a flashlight was turned on and directed to the floor. Diane Morgan then led each initiate, one by one, to the sarcophagus. When my turn came, I cleared the three-foot lip of the sarcophagus and lay down inside, my head away from where Yokar sat on the boulder. He chanted resonant Atlantean words that seemed to bounce off the walls and ceiling, if there was one, and hit my body—particularly my heart and head centers—in warm ecstatic waves. He then said in English, "This one is completed."

A flashlight guided me out and toward the opposite wall to sit and wait. As I sat, I meditated and felt like I floated off into the starry night. When everyone was initiated, we filed back down through the black corridor while Yokar closed down the energy of the pyramid. At the bottom the lights were turned back on, we disrobed, and Michael rejoined us. We had been instructed to remain silent and not to make eye contact with anyone outside the group until the following morning. I noted the time as 11:00 P.M. We would be awakened at 4:00 A.M. for the sunrise ceremony in the pyramid.

I could not sleep. I tossed and turned until 4:00. By 5:00 A.M. we were back in the pyramid, again without lights, climbing up to the King's Chamber. Once the entire group arrived in the chamber, Yokar did a Vrill transmission for all of us together to seal in the energies and patterns that had been implanted in us the night before. I felt that all of my experiences of the trip, as well as an inner knowing and strength, had now been sealed within my body. With the ceremony complete, flashlights were turned on, and I saw, all around me, faces as radiant as mine. We had all been touched by spirit.

Three days earlier, Juan Li had asked Renu to marry him and she had agreed. They requested that Yokar perform the marriage ceremony in the King's Chamber after the initiations. Yokar acquiesced. Candles were lit along the edge of the sarcophagus, and we witnessed a couple married

Author meditating on priest's rock day after initiation.

by an Atlantean priest for the first time in ten thousand years. The occasion was joyous and added an additional warm emotion to the morning.

On leaving the King's Chamber I noted that it was not

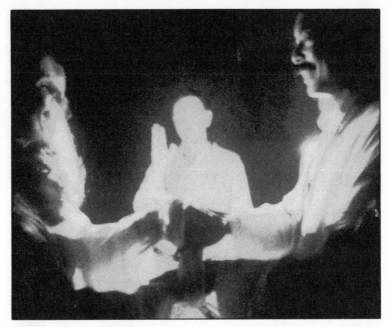

Michael in trance as Yokar performs the marriage of Renu and Juan.

such a large space and that the ceiling was solid stone, totally different impressions from those of the previous night. As we stepped out of the Great Pyramid at sunrise, we were greeted by a group of about fifty Japanese tourists, all dressed in white, performing salutations to the sun. What a glorious beginning!

9 Cleanup

I come to burn through your illusions.
—Yokar

Back in Santa Fe by March, I reconnected with friends, my men's group, and Kayo, my "little brother." I was part of the Big Brothers/Little Brothers organization of Santa Fe and got a lot of satisfaction out of being a mentor to a sixteen-year-old. In Egypt I had bought Kayo an Arab scarf, similar to Yasser Arafat's, an item not usually found in the Mexican-American community.

Now that I had stopped trading, I dedicated my time to writing and becoming physically prepared for my Tibetan journey. I started my exercise program by doing three- to four-hour hikes at elevations of eight- to nine-thousand feet. When it was too muddy outdoors, I worked out for an hour on my Nordic Track. March and April in Santa Fe are times of transition. Most days are sunny and warm, and other days there are blizzards. During this period I tried to find a travel agency to set up a personalized tour for Khenpo, Gerry Gelb, and me. I soon learned that the only way to get a visa for Tibet was through an approved agency of the Chinese government. When I contacted several American and English agencies who specialized in Tibetan tours, I was led up blind alleys. They would only consider packaged tours that involved trekking or tourism, neither of which interested me. I specifically wanted a tour, as outlined by Khenpo, that would cover Lhasa, its surroundings, the Drikung Thil Monastery, Terdom Nunnery, and the area near it. I was becoming exasperated. I called Khenpo for a suggestion.

He had no contacts with travel agents in Tibet nor any specifics in the United States. I changed the subject.

"By the way, Khenpo, the channeler I met in Egypt said that I would shake hands with death in Tibet."

Khenpo laughed uproariously.

"What's so funny?"

Between giggles he blurted out, "What a marvelous opportunity."

I thanked him for his good humor and hung up the phone. I was getting the message: to meet death I had to know my innermost depths.

Through mutual friends I met Julie, an author of shamanistic books. She invited me for lunch, which turned out to be a most delicious meal, for she was a cordon-bleu chef. Our conversation roamed from shamanism to spirituality and I proceeded to tell her about the events leading up to my proposed Tibetan trip. Besides being a shaman, writer, and chef, Julie was also a psychic. She looked at me with her big brown eyes and said, "Spirit says you will die in Tibet. You have too much unfinished business. You have caused great suffering emotionally, and you have been unfair in your financial dealings with your wife."

I was stunned and once again felt an ice pick jammed into my shoulder blade. Yokar's words about yielding and preparation came to my mind. I needed to do a lot more than just get in shape physically. To prepare for death, I needed to clean up my life emotionally, spiritually, and in every other aspect. After I returned home and meditated, Julie's words struck even harder. I decided to actualize the cleanup.

In the fall of 1990, when Bette and I had been preparing to move to Santa Fe, I had already formed a question in my mind as to whether we would stay together. I knew that the state of New Mexico had an equal-asset split in cases of divorce. Therefore, as strong remnants of my wheeling and dealing days in the commodity world remained, I had forced upon Bette a post-nuptial contract. In the event of our divorce, this contract would give 70 percent of our assets to me and 30 percent of them to Bette.

I now knew in my heart that this contract was not fair. If I was truly to yield to the life force, I needed to be open and fair in all my dealings and let go of my attachments to materialism. Bette and I were still seeing each other from time to time, as neither of us had developed another relationship. I told her I wanted to perform a ritual together and burn the document. She told me the contract was my creation and, therefore, in my dominion to destroy. She would have no part of the ritual. So one cold night when I was home alone, I took the contract out of the safe and threw it onto a roaring fire. The wind howled outside. The fire crackled, and sparks flew up against the screen as the document disintegrated. I sat mesmerized, watching large sums of money go up in smoke.

I drifted into a meditative trance. The history of my relationship with Bette unfolded in my mind's eye: My falling in love with her on seeing her picture in the freshman yearbook. Our courting and eventual marriage. Our having children together. The emotional dances we performed as I fought my way up in the gladiator's arena of the international coffee world. My inability to understand her difficulty with our separations each time I traveled abroad, and the stiffness of our reunions upon my return. My need to control and possess everything in my life. Her need for security. And now, my understanding that I needed to let go of everything and jump into the void, lose my control and possessiveness, and surrender to the life force.

I also understood Bette's need to be on her own—to rely on her own abilities and self—if we were ever to meet again as new lovers. At this very moment, I developed an understanding of one of my favorite questions: "Who owns what?" Did my material objects, preconceived ideas, and habits own me, or did I own them? I finally understood deep inside that the things that owned me were my attachments—the things I could not let go of. I decided to begin divesting myself of the material objects and patterns that possessed me.

As I sat in front of the fire, I missed Bette. Or was I only being nostalgic and missing female companionship? The fire was dying down. I realized my monkey mind had overtaken my serenity. I let go of the thoughts and reconnected with my deep feelings of equanimity and joy over destroying my own apparent advantage.

Over the next year and a half, in addition to burning this document, I sold the Long Island house as well as my ultimate, forty-four-foot, racing cruising boat. I restructured my mental and emotional attachments. I still had beautiful material objects, but I was clear about who owned what. I was clear that I could let go of them without a second thought.

The evening after I burned my contract with Bette, I received a totally unexpected call from J.W., a Taoist I had met the previous summer at a Master Chia retreat. He had sold his interest in an automotive supply business and become an active Taoist teacher in the Detroit area.

"Hello Claude, this is The Professor, J.W. from Detroit. How are you doing?"

"Great, J.W. What brings me the honor of your call?"

"You've been on my mind. I was doing my practices this morning and was deep in meditation when two names came up, yours and Gerry Gelb's. I thought it was an unusual combination. Therefore, I'm calling both of you to see if there is a link. You're the first."

"Well, the only link I can think of is that he's planning to join me on a trip to Tibet."

"Really. What's in Tibet?"

And once again I told my story of the events leading to my decision to go to Tibet.

"That's it," J.W. said. "I think I need to join you. I don't know anything about Buddhism, but they tell me these monks can walk on air. I want to meditate on this further. Would it be okay for me to join your expedition?"

I had always found that J.W. tended to go to extremes in all his opinions and actions.

"Sure," I said. "Anyone who gets the call is welcome. It's not within my purview to stop a spiritual quest."

"Great. I will be back to you with confirmation. In the meantime I'd like to know when, how long, and how much?"

I gave him as many details as I could, considering that I still did not have any firm commitment from a travel agent.

A week later I called Gerry Gelb to see how he was doing. He told me he had spoken to J.W. and was glad J.W. was joining me, because he had decided not to come. Since his return from Thailand, Gerry had become involved with his synagogue and particularly with the kabala and Zoharism. He was now convinced that the kabala was his path and therefore saw no need to go to Tibet. I wished him luck on his journey. The number of travelers in Tibet remained constant at three, although the players were changing.

Late in April, Michael Morgan came to visit Santa Fe and do some channeling. He joined me at my men's group, where Yokar answered questions posed by those present. Several private sessions were generated from the experience. Michael and I often talked late into the night. One evening I took the opportunity to ask him where I could purchase the music tape he used for our climb up to the King's Chamber.

Michael answered, "That's an impossibility. I'll tell you why. I was instructed by Yokar to go to the tape section of Sam Goody's store in Manhattan."

Yokar had told him to walk up to the case and buy the tape sticking out in the third row. The tape was called "Ancient Peruvian Music," and it had the name of the composer and an address and phone number on the label. Michael bought it and took it home. Later he played the tape for a friend who fell in love with it and went back to Sam Goody to purchase another copy. He couldn't find it, and the store claimed they had never had such a tape; it was not on their computer list. When Michael tried to contact the composer, he was informed that no such address existed and that the telephone number had never been issued.

The mystery of Egypt continued. The next day I had a private session with Yokar.

"Greetings to you. How may we be of service?"

"Changes are happening rapidly in my life on all levels, Yokar."

"Yes, it is normal. The experiences in Egypt are taking hold."

"Tell me, Yokar, I want to go to Tibet but I'm having difficulty finding a travel agent willing to set up a private tour. Any suggestions?"

"Yes. You have decided in your mind that this trip and everything related to it should be complicated. Go back to the philosophy you held in your deal-making days. 'Define your meatball' as you used to say. Go after it. I assure you, my friend, that you will find exactly what you want if you flow with the life force and simplify your needs."

"All right, my simple need is to find an approved agency to take us to the sites as defined by Khenpo. By the way, is Khenpo the one that owes me a life on the journey?"

"No comment."

"What about J.W.? Does it make sense for him to join us on this trip?"

"Moment, please. Yes, I see that he has an issue that he must deal with. As far as you are concerned, my friend, I must tell you it will make no difference how many companions join you. When the time for your trial comes, you will be alone. Each one of them for one reason or another will not be with you. I repeat, you will be alone in your trial; perhaps one other person will be present and may not speak your language."

"Yokar, you're giving me extreme anxiety."

"And well you should be anxious, for you have not finished your preparation. You still have 'cleanup' as you call it."

"Well, I'm getting prepared physically, and I cleaned

up some unsavory financial issues with Bette. What else is there to clean up?"

"Your truth—your truth in words, emotions, and every aspect of your life."

"Yokar, what do you mean by truth? I am truthful."

"No, you are not. It is as much a lie to avoid saying something as it is to say it in a lie. You are soon planning to leave for your house by the shore, are you not?"

"Yes."

"And are you not planning to see other women, to open yourself to other relationships?"

"Yes."

"Have you told Bette?"

"No. I don't see that I should. We're separated."

"You still see her on an intimate basis, do you not?"

"Yes."

"Then you must tell her the brutal truth of your intentions, for she still holds out hope of your getting back together. You have a free will, and it is yours to decide how many relationships you want to have. However, in doing so you must be truthful with each person as to your relationships with the others. The decision of whether Bette wants to see you or not becomes hers. If she accepts your actions, that is her decision, not yours. You will have relinquished control and thereby will flow with the life force. To be partners with the Most High means to speak your truth at all times no matter the consequences."

"Yokar, you're a hell of a task master."

"I am of the fire, my friend. I come to burn through your illusions."

"But Yokar, some truths are subjective. What then?"

"When that is the situation, you can tell the person it is your personal view, but there is nothing subjective in this case. You must call Bette after this session and speak your truth. Speak your truth for the rest of your existence. It is difficult. No one on your planet likes to hear or tell the truth, but you must return to it."

We went on to other subjects, and eventually Michael

came back to his body. The next day Michael went back East, and I met with Bette. She looked attractive, but I could tell our separation was taking its toll, and I was not there to bring good news.

"Bette, as you know, I'm planning to go to Sag Harbor for the summer, and in doing so I intend to leave myself open to new relationships."

She took a deep breath and then sighed. "I figured as much when you told me your plans."

Her tone was flat, and I was not sure what to say next. I felt a deep cleansing going through me for having spoken the truth. Trying to ease the mood, I said, "Why don't I go in July and you can take the rest of the time?"

Her expression was one of disgust as she responded, "I have no intention of going out there and sleeping in the same bed where you have had affairs."

I felt my chest and heart sinking. I broke down and cried uncontrollably. Bette put her arms around me and I sobbed in the crook of her neck, my body shaking. I slowly pulled away, holding both her hands at arms' length; then I let go and walked out.

A week later I received a call from one of the American travel agencies with whom I had been working. The caller told me they could not organize a private tour of Tibet, but suggested that I contact Tibet International Sports Travel, or TIST, directly in Lhasa. She gave me their phone and telex numbers. I drafted a telex and contacted my old company, because I knew they still had telex machines. The company forwarded the message to TIST, and within forty-eight hours I had a reply. Indeed the Tibetan travel organization could accommodate my requirements. From that point on, the logistics of the trip became much easier, and things quickly came together.

I had ten days left in Santa Fe before I would head east to Long Island. I wanted to spend time alone in the mountains, climb to higher altitudes as the snow melted, and perform the summer solstice ceremony that Yokar had taught me.

In Yokar's teachings, the solstices and equinoxes are
moments in time when you can do rituals to connect you
more deeply to your own energies in relation to the
surrounding world. You can ask the spirit world, through
prayer or by any other method, for help or guidance in
your journey through life. The solstices and equinoxes are
times of greater openings to spirit, each one representing
a different energy. The spring equinox is a time to plant
new seeds in life—to define and ask the spirit world for
help with your new intentions, new paths, or new begin-
nings of any sort. The summer solstice is the time of
greatest light, the time to fully develop the intentions you
set in the spring, to bring to fruition your new paths, your
new endeavors. The fall equinox is a time of letting go,
and the winter solstice a time of introspection.

All these ceremonies are performed alone, in an outdoor
spot special to you, and at a time of greatest energies
relative to the time of year. The summer solstice ceremony
is performed facing south at high noon, the time of greatest
sun (or positive propulsive) energy. If the moon is waxing
at the time of the solstice, the ceremony is performed on
the solstice itself. But if the moon is waning, the ceremony
is performed at the full moon just before the solstice.

The spring equinox ceremony is done at sunrise, facing
east, just as the sun breaks the horizon. Do the ceremony
on the day of the equinox if the moon is waxing. If the
moon is waning, do the ceremony at the full moon on the
closest date prior to the equinox.

The fall equinox ceremony is performed at sundown,
just as the sun drops below the horizon, facing west. The
moon conditions need to be the same as those for the two
ceremonies discussed above. Use the fall ritual to let go
of emotions, attitudes, behaviors, or physical things.

The winter solstice is performed at the time of greatest
darkness, facing north. For people just starting energy work,
the ritual is best done at sundown under a waning, or
decreasing, moon. Or, it can be done the day of the new
moon prior to the solstice if the moon is waxing on the

solstice. For those used to meditation, the ritual should be done at midnight under the same moon conditions. This time of greatest darkness, yin, or negative attractive energy, is best used for introspection. It is a time to review the past year, past issues and blockages, and to ask spirit to help you in understanding yourself and the blockages so they can be worked on. In the spring, the process starts all over again.

The requirements for each ceremony are: fire, from either a lighter or matches; water, spring or pure; air, all around you; metal, a needle or pin; earth, the ground or a rock; soul/spirit, your blood drawn by needle prick; and any object, picture, or list on which you might feel it necessary to focus your intention.

The ceremony should be performed alone, because energies invoked during them will last for eternity. If another person is present, your spirit will be tied to the other person's spirit for eternity. If, in the letting-go or fall-equinox ceremony, you let go of another person, the letting go will be for eternity. Personally, I do not find myself enlightened enough to know my future lives with others, so I do the ceremonies alone.

In performing the ritual, center yourself by drumming or sitting in silence; listening to your own heartbeat is another good method. Once centered, pay your respects to the spirit of the land you are standing on. This can be done with a simple internal acknowledgment or by putting out a small offering, like a cookie, as the Tibetans do. The next step is to call in the spirits of the four directions.

Because each ceremony culminates in its own particular direction, you need to begin the ritual in the direction that will orient you properly. In the spring, start the ritual facing south and turn to your right until you face east for the sunrise. In the summer, start facing west so you will end up facing south. In the fall, start facing north and end facing west. In the winter, start facing east and end facing north.

Begin the call by drumming, rattling, or simply calling in the spirit of the direction required for the ceremony.

Ask the spirit to acknowledge and sanctify what you are about to do and clearly state your purpose and intent. Be quiet, listen, and look in the direction you are calling for confirmation from the spirit world. This may manifest in the form of an animal noise or appearance, or you may feel a strong internal sensation. Whatever form the confirmation takes, mirror it back to the spirit world in thanks and acknowledgment.

Now turn right to the next direction and repeat the procedure until you are facing the appropriate compass point for the ritual. Do your final call. Be fully present and hold the intention of what you want from the spirit world. Your offering to the spirit world is the intent with which you ask for a favor. Now seal your bargain with the spirit world by enumerating your purposes and intentions and performing the ceremony.

Use your fire—matches—to heat and disinfect the needle. Prick the end of your finger to draw a drop of blood. Pour the water over your finger to spill your blood—spirit—onto the earth. As you complete the spilling of your blood on the ground, say with full conviction, "I make this transmission to spirit. I offer my being for the purpose of transformation. By my will I do this, and by the will of the Most High." The bargain has been sealed. Sit quietly for a few moments and take in everything around you.

For the summer solstice of 1992, I climbed to one of my favorite rock outcroppings in the Santa Fe mountains, at about twelve thousand feet, to connect to the spirit world. I set out early, as I needed to be in my secluded spot before noon. As I performed my ceremony on the mountain, I found myself connected to the world around me: chipmunks and squirrels appeared, squawking ravens flew above me, and the wind rustled the aspen leaves. I gave recognition to each of the spirit world's acknowledgments. I deeply set my intent to keep growing and to become more conscious in each moment, and I asked the spirit world for help.

Before leaving for Sag Harbor, I wanted to do one more ritual, a shamanistic journey with my friend David Carson, coauthor of *Medicine Cards*. I had met David at a book-signing in Taos. I taught him some Taoist practices and he revealed to me the way of animal medicine and the use of the drum. I called David, told him of my plans to go to Tibet, and asked if he could guide me in some internal work. David agreed and suggested bringing Nina, his wife, along to help in my journeying.

David is a big, bearded man with blond-to-white hair and a ruddy complexion. His eyes are blue or gray, depending on whether they are stalking or reflecting his warm compassionate energy. Upon meeting him, I could not believe this man had Choctaw blood in his veins and in his youth had lived for a considerable time on Indian reservations. As our friendship developed, I came to understand that under his quiet ways lay deep knowledge of Native American spiritual medicine. Nina, a brunette with sparkling dark eyes, was a perfect complement to David's bearlike appearance.

Two weeks later we went into the hills behind Ojo Caliente, northwest of Santa Fe. Before any ritual or journeying could be done, we needed to locate a sacred space. I was drawn to a small knoll by the side of a mountain. As we climbed the knoll, we found innumerable crystal formations and abundant sagebrush. We asked permission from the elements to gather sage and crystals, and left some tobacco in thanks to the spirits of the plants and rocks. On top of the knoll was an indentation the size of a large bathtub surrounded by red rock, piñon, cedar, and budding flowers, just the right place for me to sit or lie down for my journeying. At the head of the indentation were a couple of smaller boulders that David and Nina could sit on to guide, drum, and rattle.

I placed the crystals around my sacred space, and then we proceeded to smudge each other and my space with the sage. From this vantage point we could see the snow-capped Sangre de Cristo mountains to the east and the Ojo

River below us. Far to the north, we could see the out-croppings of Colorado. To the west were the Jemez Mountains, and to the south, the red and green terrain of Los Alamos and Santa Fe. The sky was a clear, clear blue.

The first order of the day was to call the spirits of the four directions, followed by Mother Earth and Father Sky. My first journey was to find my totem power animal for support and guidance. This type of journey involved going into the underworld. I would go down a long dark tunnel until an opening occurred. The hole to the tunnel would be an anthill hole, a log hole, or a cave, whatever the drumming and rattling would bring me.

David felt that because of my meditation and tantric practices I should do the journey falling backward. Backward in Native American medicine is very sacred. Many American Indians have two names: their family names, and their vision-quest or medicine names, reflecting their inner truths or guidance—at a particular time or for life. Any American Indian with a name like Falling Backward or Falls off a Horse is special, and is often a medicine man, or shaman. To fall backward is to take a leap into the void; it is to trust that the Great Spirit, or life force, will catch and keep you safe.

I agreed with David's suggestion, although I was definitely uneasy about falling backward in the spirit world. I lay down in the indentation while David and Nina sat on the rocks a few feet from my head. David started drumming and Nina began rattling. David had placed a bandanna over my eyes, and all was darkness. Colors, shapes and figures tumbled in my mind's eye. I let go and fell backward. Suddenly I found myself tumbling downward in a conelike funnel. At the bottom, I was met by an American Indian child in a loincloth. I was still unsteady and, crawling on my hands and knees, followed him into a passage. We went down a steep incline and came to an opening, but he motioned me down further. A second opening appeared and I found myself in a clearing of a tropical forest. Suddenly my young Indian guide turned into an old man.

He led me out of the clearing into the foliage. We came across a black panther, an old friend from a meditation; I acknowledged his presence and moved on. When I found myself in the deepest part of the jungle, my guide disappeared. I breathed deeply, sensing a presence. I looked up and saw a huge boa constrictor draped over a large limb, looking directly at me. I have always feared snakes. I stared back at the boa and asked, "Are you supposed to be my totem animal?"

He opened his mouth and spoke clearly. "Yes. Why are you astonished? You have developed the same strengths as I. You became a force to be reckoned with in business. You could have used your strength to crush your opposition, much as I can; yet you didn't. Wisdom is having great strength without using it except for ultimate good. Come, climb up here and I will show you."

I was fascinated and climbed up without hesitation. He then went on, "I will let down one of my coils—go sit on it."

I did as I was told. Then Boa swung me, like on a swing, in his great coil; another coil served as a back rest. I felt like an infant in Mother Earth's embrace. The smells of the jungle were humid and earthy. A voice from below called up, "Time to go." My old Indian guide was motioning me on. I thanked Boa and rejoined my guide. When I reached the connection to the tunnel I was suddenly catapulted back up to ground level, standing on both feet. My mind was still wheeling when I heard a change in the drumbeat indicating my journey was coming to an end. I came to and took off the bandanna. David and Nina were smiling at me.

Nina said, "You must have had a special journey—butterflies flew over you, and a red-tailed hawk or eagle circled high up for a while."

David added, "And there was a gray squirrel who poked its head over the rock by your feet." All these animals had medicine meanings: Butterfly represented "transformation"; Hawk was the "messenger"; Eagle represented "spirit";

Squirrel was "gathering." I told David and Nina about my journey.

As defined in David's book, Snake is the medicine of transmutation. As later elucidated by Yokar, Snake represents wisdom, with the ability to strike deep at the core of issues. Both meanings resonated within my soul.

My journeys continued, with David's guidance and drumming and Nina's rattling. I worked on the male medicine animal of each chakra. Then I identified the female medicine animal of each chakra, which we found by moving down to the river bank, for the water's female, intuitive help. The next day we did some deeper work, culminating in a journey of my own death. At the end of this journey David asked me, "How was your death in Tibet?"

"David, you asked me to see my own death without specifying Tibet. I did not see my death in Tibet at all. In fact, I saw two possible deaths. In one I was being rushed in an ambulance to a modern hospital. As the surgeons were about to operate, I decided I did not want to stick around and left my body. In the other death scenario, I saw myself deep in peaceful meditation, and I simply decided to leave my body. I did not feel terror, excitement, or joy in either case but was a calm witness to my own death. Very settling actually. Nothing to do with Tibet."

"Well, that's good. Do you want to do one more journey to Tibet and see what comes up?"

"Yes, let's do that."

I lay down in the indentation. David started drumming and Nina began rattling. The sounds were primal. I went deep and decided to shoot my energy out of my crown, and move forward to Tibet. I found myself connecting through airplanes and then, suddenly, I was in a monastery high up in the mountains. As I visualized the monastery, I heard a deep, modulated droning. My monkey mind came back in and thought I was hearing a plane overhead. I was annoyed that the sound had disturbed my journey. However, the droning did not go away. It accentuated into clearly defined rhythms. I let go of the present and, with my monkey mind suspended, returned to my journey. It dawned on me that I was hearing Tibetan monks chanting. I was being invited back to a world I once knew, a world of many monks in orange robes chanting in a tall, columned hall. The monastery was cool, and the resonant chanting continuous. I drifted off. The chanting stopped, and I slowly came back to the New Mexican mountains. I opened my eyes and saw David and Nina smiling down at me.

"Well, how was it?"

I smiled. "You are not going to believe this." I recounted my journey, and they were both quite moved. We drummed, gave thanks to the spirit world, and came down the mountain.

Shortly thereafter, I flew to New York City on my way to Sag Harbor. I visited with family and friends, and joined most of the Egyptian group one evening for a Yokar session. Before the session I had dinner with John Paccione, Mike Winn, and others. We brought each other up to date on our lives. John Paccione had never heard about my various experiences, from my connection with Sai Baba to my trip to Tibet. He was fascinated.

"Why don't things like that happen to me?"

"John, they do. Look around you—there was your sunlamp experience, the Egyptian initiations, and many other experiences."

"Yes, but I want something more dramatic."

"The drama is within yourself. Just be in touch with it, and you will perceive the miracles."

The following morning I went to Sag Harbor. Two days later, early on a Monday morning, I got a call from John. "Claude," he said, "I would like to join you in Tibet."

"Sure, with pleasure. I'm going to need all your passport information pretty quickly to telex to Lhasa for visa permission. It is now mid-June and we leave in three months. Also, you need to get into some sort of physical condition, and get equipment, shots, and preventative medication."

I could tell he was beaming over the phone. He said,

"Great, give me the details. I really feel I'm going there for you."

"What do you mean?"

"I have a feeling that, because of your heart, I'm supposed to be with you. Perhaps I'm the one who owes you a life?"

I did not have that feeling but chose not to say so.

"Who knows? In any event I would truly enjoy your companionship. Your sense of humor will be a great complement to J.W.'s seriousness. Speaking of that, he is going to be at Master Chia's retreat in Phoenicia, New York. I think it would be a good idea to drive up together so you can meet him."

Later that summer we took two days off together and traveled to Phoenicia. John and J.W. got along well. We took a picture together. J.W. was in the center. His dark eyes, black hair, and beard reminded me of Bludo in the Popeye comics. J.W. had been a football player in college and looked like he could carry a mountain. The Tibetans would come to dub him "The Yak."

As a Scorpio, I felt in my element when surrounded by the water at Sag Harbor. I settled into my environment and did some deep meditations. After a week I realized that I did not want to confuse my preparation and cleansing for Tibet by initiating new relationships. I felt comfortable in my total truth and decided to tell Bette of my new decision. Our phone conversation was intimate, and I felt a great love for her. We decided we would spend the month of August together at the seashore, giving our relationship of thirty-two years a final try. Our month together turned out to be a mixture of delights—playing tennis, sailing, and making love— offset by unpleasant old records we played at each other. We could not transcend our past and our differences, and so we parted once again to walk our own paths. My head was now being propelled toward the Tibetan journey only twenty days away. I no longer wanted to think about relationships.

Some months later I successfully sold my Long Island house using the fall-equinox ceremony. However, I found I needed to be clear about my intentions, for the sale was not consummated until I was willing to let go of what the house represented. I went from room to room, collecting my memories from each room and then letting them go. Eventually I let go of the entire property. The house was under contract within a week.

Once I was back in Santa Fe, time flew, and the group coalesced. John Paccione arrived, then J.W., and finally Khenpo. Before Khenpo's arrival, John Paccione and I taught J.W. how to do the fall-equinox ceremony. We spent ten days acclimating to the altitude. I began by taking the group on hikes at around nine thousand feet. Then we swiftly jumped to eleven and twelve thousand feet. I felt perfectly fine. I had played aggressive tennis all summer and taken long barefoot walks on the beach. My comrades were not as physically prepared, and I reminded them that our minimum altitude in Tibet would be in Lhasa at twelve thousand feet. We kept hiking, and by the day before our departure, we all felt great.

10 Katmandu/Lhasa

*Be conscious of the rotting flesh,
as yours will be some day.*
—Khenpo Gyaltsen

We arrived in Katmandu, Nepal, on September 18, 1992. It was 10:00 A.M. and already the temperature was about eighty degrees. J.W. immediately made a comment about all the equipment he had brought. He had arrived in Santa Fe without any gear, which had annoyed me. I had not felt that outfitting him was my responsibility. Earlier, concerned about everyone's comfort, I had sent him a three-page list of suggested items, from boots to medicines. He had bought nothing. So we had shopped in Santa Fe for J.W.'s equipment, including a sleeping bag, expedition-weight polypropylene underwear, socks, hiking boots, and all the other necessities needed for strenuous, cold conditions.

A certain tension had started building when a day of hiking was lost due to J.W.'s required shopping trip. I knew this tension would grow, for Tibet was a mysterious, high-altitude country that would test our spirits and resolve as we spent more time in close quarters. The rarefied air would influence our perceptions of reality. My experience in close quarters during offshore sailing had taught me to choose my crew carefully, for storms and life-threatening situations altered the human condition. I had seen strong men hide in their bunks, unable to function when the elements of sea and wind tore loose. I was not expecting such a scenario on this spiritual quest; on the other hand, I had not chosen my companions. I had felt that anyone who wanted to come on the journey was meant to be there.

Mr. Kalden of Tibet Travel, the TIST representative in Nepal, was at the airport to guide us through the formalities. Khenpo let the rest of us carry his extra baggage and camera; he said the Nepalese went out of their way to give Tibetan monks a difficult time. Once cleared, we were driven to the Vajra Hotel. On the way I noticed the amount of garbage along the road: plastic, vegetables, cardboard, and detritus. At four thousand feet, Katmandu was hot, humid, and very noisy.

The Vajra Hotel was like an oasis, on the outskirts of the main thoroughfares, removed from the cacophony. The main entrance was reached through a brick courtyard bordered by high walls that were covered with vines. To one side of the courtyard, surrounded by flowers, was a small altar to Ganesh, the God of Good Fortune. Inside the courtyard were little nooks, hidden between the apartment walls, where we would have breakfast served to us in the morning. Our rooms were large and airy. We had decided to rotate roommates so we would all get to know one another. I started with J.W., and John Paccione roomed with Khenpo. After checking in, we went downtown to pick up our visas and airline tickets for Tibet.

Kalden informed us he did not have the visas because TIST had never sent them. Panic. All eyes fixed on me as the responsible one. My old fear of performing less than expertly came up. I let it go. I showed Kalden the telex clearly stating that Tibet Travel would make the arrangements to have the visas in Katmandu. Kalden assured us he could reach TIST and fix the problem.

We lunched in a small restaurant in one of the back alleys of Katmandu. The city was comparable to a medieval town, its tiny, narrow streets crowded with vendors, pedestrians, cars, and bicycles. The buildings were two to four stories high, creating dim light in the streets even at high noon. We visited some shops, and I bought a red T-shirt with a black dragon on the front for Kayo. We returned to Tibet Travel to get a report. Kalden informed us that TIST was disorganized because the head man was in the hospital and his assistant on tour. He had spoken to the officer in charge at the Chinese Embassy and had arranged for the officer to work late to process our visas. I let him know where we would be dining that evening. I hoped the visas would be in hand before the next morning's early flight. We returned to the hotel, washed up, and went back to Katmandu and dinner.

At 9:45 P.M. Kalden showed up at the restaurant and said that the visas were impossible to get. TIST had mixed up all our information with that of other visitors, and none of their information corresponded to that on our passports. We would not be on the next morning's flight, and there was a question about Tuesday, as that flight was fully booked. After all the months of careful planning, I was exasperated.

Kalden assured us he would get back to TIST the following morning with all the proper information, which he would take directly from our passports. Only TIST could give permission directly to the Chinese Embassy; such permission had to come from a recognized Chinese travel agency.

The next day was Saturday, and we sat around the breakfast table feeling glum—except Khenpo, who was in his usual good humor. Our breakfast nook was a cozy corner surrounded by the high vined walls, and the early morning sun smiled down on our gathering. J.W. voiced his skepticism. "This does not look good. What do we do if we don't get on the Tuesday plane?"

John responded, "Don't be so pessimistic. We'll get our visas and be on Tuesday's plane."

Khenpo just smiled and kept eating his porridge. I reflected on the fact that J.W. always seemed ready to voice his concerns, yet did not seem to think or act in a positive fashion to resolve problems. In discussions ranging from politics to religion, he invariably suggested conspiracies or cover-ups to explain the events of history. Nothing ever seemed to work out to his liking. After breakfast we found out that all telecommunication in Katmandu had broken down, making it impossible to get through to Lhasa. Perhaps J.W. was right: there was a conspiracy preventing us from going to Tibet. Yokar had told me I would be severely tested on all levels. I decided I had to remain calm and flow with the situation.

We all went for a hike to the big stupa on the outskirts of town, a half-hour walk from the Vajra Hotel. On the way we passed a dead goat that we smelled from a hundred yards away. We covered our noses as we passed it. With sparkling eyes, Khenpo said, "This is very good for all of you. Mark the scene in your minds, as we will use it in our meditation tonight on death and impermanence. Be conscious of the rotting flesh, as yours will be some day."

I had asked Khenpo to start teaching us some meditation practices because John and J.W. had not been familiar with Buddhism. This waiting time had been perfect, so each morning and evening we had meditated and chanted together for about an hour. By Saturday evening we got confirmation from Kalden that he had contacted TIST.

The next morning, Sunday, we again had breakfast in our sunny nook by the vined brick wall. Khenpo, as usual, concentrated on his porridge. The conversation turned to politics and the news media. J.W. complained that the media really ran politics and conspired to influence the public. I felt a tension rise in me and concentrated on trying to let it pass, wishing to be like Khenpo and accept all beings. But I wanted to discover more about how J.W.'s mind worked.

"What do you mean the media conspires to influence people?"

In amazement, J.W. challenged my naiveté. He implied that all the news media of the United States—the newspapers, radio stations, TV stations—were controlled by a Jewish club. He said the Jews distorted everything to suit their purposes and that the Holocaust was Jewish Mafia propaganda perpetuated by Israel.

I could not believe my ears. I could not believe I was traveling and rooming with such a person. I was so stunned

I trembled. J.W. obviously did not have a clue about my background. Although I had been brought up as a Catholic, the religion of my father had been Judaism. My whole family had fled Belgium under the strafing of the *Luftwaffe* at the onset of World War II. I had been three and a half, and the experience was still embedded in my bones.

I retorted, "You really don't mean what you said. The horrors perpetrated on the Jews were recorded. Go see the pictures. Get into the U.S. archives. Go read something beyond the distorted reporting of the Fascists."

He was unmoved, smiled a broad grin, and jutted his head forward, beard first. He said that a few pictures of some Jews exterminated by a few Nazi zealots did not make six million dead Jews.

Khenpo kept eating his porridge, and John smiled as if enjoying the show. Yokar's words came to me: "Remember, for every surge on the light side there is a surge on the dark side. For that is how balance is kept on your planet." I did not want to be part of this discussion. I wanted to be on my spiritual quest of the lotus blossom, yet I felt my feet in the muddy quagmire. J.W.'s opinions were set in concrete, and I was not about to change them. I recentered myself, trying to feel compassion in the hope that I could follow the path of service in spite of the darkness around me. I dropped the subject but was unable to talk with ease to J.W. for a long time.

After breakfast we went to Boudhenath, a small town about an hour's drive from Katmandu and the center of Tibetan activity in Nepal. We visited the large stupa in the square and did several meditation practices in various monasteries located around town. By evening everyone was tired and on edge. Kalden reported that he had received a telex from TIST and that everything seemed to be in order, but nothing could be done until the Chinese Embassy opened on Monday morning. The big concern was whether we could get a Tuesday morning flight; it was still fully booked. I was tired and coming down with a cold. After dinner I went to bed, and as I was falling asleep, J.W.

The author in front of large stupa in Boudhealth square.

said, "You know, this whole trip is a mess. We're never going to get to Tibet."

I bolted upright in bed.

"Fuck you! We're going to Tibet if we have to go over land. I worked like hell to put all this together, and you're just standing around complaining and criticizing. Next time you put the trip together."

He was stunned by my violent reaction. He apologized and we both went to bed. Next day my ears were clogged, and I decided to nurse myself all day so that I would be able to fly. That evening Kalden confirmed our visas. We now needed to get on the next morning flight. There was no way we were going to wait another four days.

We arrived at the airport early, and Kalden pulled a fast one by hitching our unconfirmed tickets to another passenger's confirmed ticket. The plane was jammed, but we were on it. Lunch on China Southwest Airways consisted of a boiled egg, a pack of cookies, and two chocolate bars. We crossed the snowcapped Himalayas, a spectacular sight against the dark blue skies.

The plane was full of Tibetan monks from all parts of the world. They were journeying to Tibet for the confirmation of the seventeenth Karmapa. The sixteenth Karmapa had died of cancer in the United States. He had been the first Tibetan high holy man to travel to Native American reservations. He had given teachings to the Hopi that had been very similar to some ancient Hopi spiritual practices. Part of the Hopi prophecy involved the coming of holy men, in red hats, from the East, to renew spirituality. When the sixteenth Karmapa had died, he had left a letter, not to be opened for nine years, predicting when he would reincarnate, where he could be found, and the names of his parents. The letter had recently been opened, and six months prior to our arrival, the seventeenth Karmapa had been found. He was an eight-year-old boy, just as described in the letter. I had seen a picture of this seventeenth reincarnation and had been amazed at the child's eyes. As we flew over the mountain peaks, I reflected that with luck we might see the new Karmapa.

I had prepared for this trip in every aspect. Now, as I felt the spiritual journey gaining momentum, I knew I did not want to play tour director in Tibet. I was going to let John and J.W. fend for themselves. (Khenpo was, in part, my responsibility because I was financing his way as our guide.) I determined that from this point on I was a pilgrim on a journey of awe and joy.

Our plane came careening down from the Himalayan

heights and bounced twice on the runway—thirty-foot bounces. The Lhasa airport and surroundings were bleak. The passengers were herded to waiting buses and driven to a huge hall where the formalities of entering Tibet took two hours. At the exit we were met by our TIST guide, Tsedor, and a driver. Our vehicle was an old Japanese land cruiser. We packed in, Khenpo in front with guide and driver, and the rest of us in back. This was to be the format for the entire trip. Lhasa was two hours away from the airport, and the road was dusty, rocky, and bumpy. Except for a few hundred feet on either side of the Brahmaputra River, the surroundings were stark and without vegetation. The mountains were brown, gray, and treeless.

We arrived at the Himalaya Hotel and, after surveying the poor conditions, informed our guide that we wanted to move to the Holiday Inn. Everyone agreed, and once again I found myself playing tour guide and negotiating. Tsedor called his boss, Mr. Tao, who balked due to the increased cost. I pointed out that we had lost three days due to the visa mess-up, and they owed us the difference. After a half hour we shook hands on a deal—no cost to us, no rebate from them—and we moved to the Holiday Inn. Compared to the alternatives, it was a true haven of food and lodging. We retired early, but I found sleep difficult. My heart was beating fast and my head was whirling; there was quite a difference between living at twelve thousand feet and hiking for a few hours at that altitude near Santa Fe. The next morning my head was still whirling at the crown. My brain felt as if the circuitry was being reoriented, as it had been in Egypt, although without the laughter.

We had breakfast in a large, cafeteria-style dining hall. Khenpo and I were able to find a private corner, and I discussed my condition with him.

"Most likely it's the altitude," he said. "But possibly other forces are at work, as you are going through changes."

"I feel at times that I might faint or black out. Should I go with that feeling and see what happens?"

"No, I don't think so. You should try and retain consciousness at all times."

I was reminded of an incident that occurred in Santa Fe, a few weeks earlier. Michael Morgan and his wife, Diane, were visiting during his lecture tour. One morning while they were still sleeping, I left the house to get blood drawn as part of my physical checkup before the trip. After three vials of blood were taken, I fainted. I was unconscious longer than normal, and my body started jerking. The doctor in charge of the blood labs became concerned. He called the medics and wanted me transferred to the emergency room at the hospital. He felt that my jerking while unconscious was a spasm and that I was comatose for too long. When I came to, sweating profusely, I assured him that I would be fine and refused to go to the hospital. Forty-five minutes passed before I had the strength to get up and drive home. I found Michael and Diane eating breakfast and told them what had happened. I requested a session with Yokar. During the session, I asked Yokar what the blackout was about.

"Yes, we apologize, but we had to do some work on your head before you went to Tibet. You will be exposed to unusual vibrations and need to be programmed to assimilate them. We thought that inducing you to have a blood test might be an easy way to perform our work without causing undue concern. We hope it has not caused too much of an inconvenience."

"Yokar, this is a hell of a way to treat somebody who is supposedly working for the Most High. Why not give me a warning, and I could work with you?"

"You are too much in your head as it is. You get in our way. Please be assured we know what we are doing. Just relax and allow. You must learn to allow, and you will reach the point where you are supposed to be, without your interactive mind. As far as being partners with the Most High, we have told you before that it will be a difficult road and that there is no turning back."

Now, in Lhasa, I decided that whatever was happening in my head must be allowed.

At 9:30 in the morning our driver, land cruiser, and guide, Tsedor, were waiting for us. Tsedor was tall and thin with a typical Tibetan dark complexion. He was very laconic. Khenpo explained the trip to him, giving him information and directions with respect to our movements. The only requirement was a forty-eight-hour advisory for long-distance changes because police travel permits needed to be arranged. In this context I explained to Khenpo that I would like to see the new Karmapa, if possible, before we left Lhasa for the Drikung area.

We all agreed that on Friday, September 25, we would travel to the Tsurpu monastery where the new Karmapa was living. Tsedor would make the arrangements. We left in the land cruiser to visit the Jokhang temple in the center of Lhasa. As we drove I was conscious of the bleakness of Lhasa and its surroundings. All the buildings were gray, the mountain was a dull brown, and the river valley was composed of a beige-gray sandy soil. The only relief was the colorful dress of the 50 percent of the population that was Tibetan. The Chinese, for the most part, wore either gray or blue.

We pulled up to the Jokhang temple and were engulfed in the smoke of burning offerings a hundred yards in front of the massive central doors. The temple was centrally located in the Tibetan market, Borkhar Square area, and had been the rallying symbol for many demonstrations and uprisings against the Chinese. Security was apparent. Several Chinese security squad trucks were strategically parked near the square. The square was a beehive of activity with vendors, villagers, and monks intermingling. Borkhar Square included the temple, houses, and other structures located behind it. It was equivalent in size to four city blocks. A cobblestone road went around the entire edifice, with rows of houses and low buildings on the opposite side bustling with Tibetans in their colorful robes and coats. Before entering the temple we walked around the entire complex, which included all the Borkhar Square's buildings. According to strict Tibetan belief, to earn merit, one had to circumambulate the entire holy site, meaning we had to circle it clockwise, from left to right. We walked up to the temple entrance with all the pilgrims. These worshippers carried either prayer wheels, which were in continual motion, or yak butter lamps.

To enter the front door we had to step over prostrating bodies. The stones in front were smooth, the result of full-body prostrations performed by millions of devotees over the eleven centuries of the temple's existence. Once inside the Jokhang temple's dark, thick, six-to-eight-foot walls, I recognized the familiar odor of burning ghee in the butter lamps. There were a few sparse light bulbs; otherwise, the light came from the butter lamps and our own flashlights. We visited room after room filled with statues of buddhas, friendly and wrathful deities, bodhisattvas, gurus, and enlightened beings. We left offerings of money, khatas (white scarves), and various personal items. The depth of devotion exhibited by the hundreds of pilgrims was overwhelming. Their clothes were dirty, earth-caked, and tattered, but their poverty was no detraction to their devotion. Many of them bowed to Khenpo and asked for his blessing.

The energy of the Jokhang temple overwhelmed me and set the tone for the entire trip. Coming out to a platform into the sunlight and the deep blue skies, my eyes teared up and I felt transported to ancient times. I looked over and noticed John standing next to me with tears flowing down his cheeks. We smiled and embraced each other, unashamed of our emotions. Khenpo was smiling a sly knowing smile; his eyes sparkled. J.W. looked bewildered. He turned to me and said, "Claude, if I don't visit another site, the Jokhang temple has made this trip worthwhile. I feel the energy of creation in there."

After leaving the temple, Khenpo insisted we do one more circumambulation. An hour later we finally headed back to the hotel.

We had a late lunch and then went to visit the Drepung monastery. This monastery was part of the Gelugpa order and was one of the few monasteries that had not been destroyed during the Cultural Revolution. The premises were large and well kept, with many statues and a full complement of printed teachings. Later we visited the Dalai Lama's summer palace, which included a zoo and some lovely gardens. Out in the back were some old structures where Agon Rinpoche, an old friend of Khenpo, lived. The word *Rinpoche* means "precious one," and usually denotes a recognized reincarnation; Agon was a reincarnation of a famous guru who died in the early 1900s.

This was my first visit inside a Tibetan house. The interior consisted of three small rooms; outdoors was a courtyard and outside plumbing. Agon was a slight man with black, unruly hair, dark eyes and complexion, a ready smile, and an extremely humble demeanor. He invited us to sit on a cushioned old couch while Khenpo sat beside him on an elevated wood platform covered with cushions. His wife came in to offer sweets, dry yak meat, and, of course, Tibetan tea, which was black tea churned with yak butter. We gave Agon presents of secondhand clothing, particularly sweaters, brought for this express purpose.

Agon was a psychic and recognized scholar, and while we were there a constant stream of visitors came to pay him their respects. I watched the interactions with interest. For some reason Agon kept looking at me. Khenpo and he talked at length in Tibetan. I felt that something important was going on and waited for an outcome of some kind, but none materialized. We returned to the hotel and had dinner. Khenpo led us in meditation practice after supper and then we went to bed. My head was back to normal and I got a good night's sleep.

The next day we went to visit the Potala palace, the Dalai Lama's palace, which sat atop the city's highest knoll and dominated all of Lhasa. The palace had more than a thousand rooms, all of them imbued with the spiritual and physical presence of the Dalai Lama. Tibetans were only

Potala Palace as seen from Jokhang terrace.

allowed to visit the Potala palace twice a week; otherwise it was reserved for foreigners. We were there for three hours. Khenpo was constantly stopped by visitors asking questions; he was the only monk in evidence, and of course he spoke fluent English. Tourists wanted to snap a picture of him in front of their favorite statue or carving.

We walked out to one of the palace's main courtyards. A crew of about forty Tibetan workers were repairing the floor, which, as in most monasteries, was of beaten earth and stone. The workers were split into two gangs of twenty, one men, the other women. They all had long sticks at the end of which were heavy round objects covered with cloth. One gang would sing and chant enthusiastically, stomping their feet and beating the ground with their tampers, while the other group stood by and rested. After five minutes they would switch roles, all the while smiling with happiness at the privilege of working on the Dalai Lama's residence. I felt humbled to see these men and women eking out a subsistence living yet emanating such inner joy. I reflected on all my worldly possessions, and how at that moment, in the bleakness of my surroundings, I felt more connected to spirit. So much loving energy emanated from these workers that John and I again found ourselves with tears streaming down our faces. Perhaps we were more sensitive because of our chakra initiations in Egypt.

Upon leaving the Potala palace we were deluged by Tibetan women selling jewelry. They wore long dresses of heavy black cloth covered with colorful aprons in shades of orange, green, red, white, and purple, mixed with ochre. Their jet-black hair was arranged in long braids, either brought up over their heads or hanging straight down and interwoven with colorful ribbons. Many had turquoise in their hair combs or woven into their hair with ribbons. John joked with them by trying to sell them their own goods at their asking price, a trick I had used in the commodity business when a seller's asking price was out of line. We all laughed a lot, and John and I ended up buying many necklaces and bracelets as souvenirs.

That afternoon we went back to Borkhar Square around the Jokhang temple, first to visit the medical college nearby and then to browse among the stalls. The original medical college on Iron Mountain was totally destroyed by the Cultural Revolution except for one building. The new college appeared very primitive compared to colleges in the West, but it had an outstanding reputation with respect to herbal medicine. Tibetan herbal practices were very similar to Chinese herbal medicine. My own Chinese herb doctor in Santa Fe, although of Chinese training, got most of his important herbs from the Tibetan area.

After seeing the college we continued our walk along Borkhar Square, getting an idea of the items we might want to buy when we came back. I was looking for a hand-painted tanka of Chenrezi. A tanka was a painting surrounded by ornate cloth that could be rolled up like a scroll on a stick. I had always been attracted to Chenrezi, the entity of compassion, and was even more so after seeing Doug channel him. I hoped to find a tanka in triptych that would include the other two entities of total compassion: Manjushri, carrying the flaming sword of wisdom that cuts through illusion; and Vajrapani, the black entity surrounded by fire, representing the power of action in compassion. Like the example of the Dalai Lama, such a triptych would illustrate that compassion by itself was meaningless unless accompanied by wisdom and action.

No one at the stalls had such a tanka. With Khenpo translating for me, I finally found a man who promised that one would be made in about ten days time. I kept my fingers crossed, hoping that indeed I would find this tanka on the last days of our trip. All of us bought some khatas, or traditional white scarves, for our journey, as tomorrow we would travel to Tsurpu and then on Saturday to Drikung. We each purchased at least six khatas to present as marks of respect at shrines or to give to living teachers whom we would meet. That evening we had an early dinner at the Holiday Inn and then a meditation with Khenpo.

Early the next morning we left on our three-hour trip to Tsurpu monastery, fifty miles away. The drive was a slow, rough, gradual climb, along a river valley between towering, sixteen-thousand-foot mountains. The valley became greener as we climbed, and we passed grazing yaks and millet fields in the midst of being harvested. The road was packed with pilgrims on their way to the confirmation celebration of the seventeenth Karmapa two days hence. As we slowly jostled past them, the pilgrims bowed and stuck their tongues out, particularly to Khenpo, whom they considered a high attained lama.

Sticking out the tongue dated back to the old Bon (or Bonpa) religion that predated Buddhism's arrival in Tibet. The Bon religion had two factions: a light, or good side, currently represented to a great extent by Dzogchen, as taught by Namkhai Norbu; and a dark side, represented by black magic. In centuries past, those practicing the dark side had black dots on their tongues. Therefore, the custom evolved of people proving they followed the path of light by exposing their undotted tongues. The bowing was a show of respect. When in close quarters, a pilgrim would always bow lower than the greater attained person. The ultimate experience for devotees was to bow to highly attained lamas and touch the crowns of their heads to the lamas' crowns, thereby obtaining some of their wisdom.

At times our land cruiser moved so slowly that the devotees came to Khenpo's open window, bowed with their hands in prayer, and touched crowns. Watching all these farmers, monks, and other pilgrims in disheveled clothes walking great distances because of their spiritual devotion was very moving.

We arrived at Tsurpu around noon. The monastery had been largely destroyed by the Chinese except for the main building, which had been refurbished and was in good condition. As we pulled into the courtyard, our vehicle was surrounded by monks and pilgrims, sunbaked and smiling, some with only a few teeth. Khenpo stepped out, showing his broad, warm smile. They all bowed, wanting to connect to his crown, wanting to touch him, wanting his blessing. We stepped back and watched these very sensitive devotions. My tears of joy and awe were hidden by my dark glasses. So were John's. J.W. was just stunned. The entire monastery was surrounded by pitched yak-hide tents and cooking fires. Love of the Buddha and dharma was everywhere.

We slowly made our way to the main entrance of the building. There we were greeted by the head abbot, from

Scene on the way up to Tsurpu monastery.

whom Khenpo requested a private audience with the seventeenth Karmapa. We were ushered into a waiting room full of stored food and cushions. Khenpo had told the head abbot that he had studied with the sixteenth Karmapa for three months, and that it was he who had suggested Khenpo move to the United States to teach the dharma. I had not realized before what a close and special connection Khenpo had to the Karmapa.

We waited twenty minutes, then were ushered into the Karmapa's private reception quarters in the penthouse. The eight-year-old Karmapa sat, Buddha-style, in resplendent robes on a cushioned platform. His head literally glowed. His coal-black eyes were soft yet penetrating. Khenpo was the first of us to pay his respect, with three full-body prostrations followed by the presentation of a khata. The Karmapa in turn blessed Khenpo by stamping the top of his head with his seal of lineage. I followed the same procedure and gave the Karmapa a bald-eagle feather, explaining that this was the symbol of the Great Spirit among Native Americans and that I was giving it to him on behalf of "all my relations."

In Native American beliefs, as in Taoism, "all my relations" meant the spirit and energy of all on the planet, including the rocks, animals, humans, oceans, and sky. The bald-eagle feather had been given to me by friends who had found the bird dead on an Arizona road. They had performed a ceremony, buried the main body, and built a medicine wheel around the eagle. They had kept the wings and tail feathers for special occasions. When they found out I was going to Tibet, they gave me the feather, asking me to leave it wherever it felt appropriate. In light of the sixteenth Karmapa's teachings to the Hopi, I felt that it was auspicious to give his reincarnation a feather reconnecting him to the American work of his previous life. The seventeenth Karmapa simply stared at the feather a few moments.

John and J.W. followed the same sequence of bowing and blessing. Each in turn gave the Karmapa a gift. Then we were ushered out of the private quarters. On the way out, we passed a long queue of pilgrims waiting for an audience.

We had a quiet and reflective picnic lunch alongside a nearby stream. The bright sun beat down and made the water glitter like diamonds. We then drove back to Lhasa, dinner, meditation practice, and sleep.

Picnic lunch along stream of Tsurpu Monastery. Khenpo sharing his lunch with Tibetan pilgrim.

11 Drikung Thil Monastery

Whoever dies is put on the sky burial.
—John Paccione

By 9:00 the next morning we were on our way to the Drikung Thil monastery. Our driver estimated the trip would take six hours, plus lunch and other breaks, although it was only 110 miles away. Five miles out of Lhasa the road became not much more than a donkey trail. As we bumped and racked along, the scenery of yaks, peasants, rivers, valleys, and mountains unrolled like a movie across my retina. I felt I was starting my real journey—the culmination of all my training, preparation, and cleansing. Drikung was specifically where Khenpo wanted to bring me.

John had once asked Khenpo why he had come on this trip, and he had replied, "I am here for Claude—to help him on his path to enlightenment."

When John told me this I was blown away. I had no expectations and was trying to keep tension to a minimum. In a way I felt like a burden, for John had made a similar statement to me when I had asked him why he was coming on the trip. I did not understand what all this meant, except that I needed to walk my truth and allow the life force to flow through me so that I could grow to serve the higher purposes for which I had incarnated.

We had with us our daypacks, which contained water and lunches for the day. Our main gear was in a truck following us; it carried our sleeping tents, cooking tent, and food for six days. At noon we stopped to eat the lunch that had been provided by the hotel, the last substantial meal we would have on the journey.

A light rain began falling as we drove up the last river valley to Drikung Thil. Soon it turned to snow. Khenpo told us, "This is a very auspicious sign. The higher forces are giving us a cleansing for our arrival."

"Isn't this a little early in the year for snow?" I asked.

"Yes. A month early. Even more auspicious."

We arrived at the base of the monastery and Tsedor, the cook, and the two drivers unloaded the gear from the truck onto the river bank.

"Khenpo," I said, "I would rather stay in the monastery if that is possible."

I knew that the Chinese had forbidden guests at monasteries because they could be troublemakers and revolutionaries. I also knew that once we were away from officialdom, arrangements could be made. From our encampment, the road up the mountain ridge led straight up. The monastery looked like blocks of rock thrown by the Most High onto the mountainside. The land cruiser struggled up the narrow steep road and arrived at the turnaround in front of the monastery's main entrance. I took my altimeter out to check the elevation; it read 14,300 feet, compared to 13,900 feet at the base camp.

We were greeted by four or five smiling young monks ranging in age from seventeen to twenty-six. They guided us up over the main monastery roof to a medium-sized room, where we sat on cushioned pallets against the four walls. Khenpo asked if we could stay in the monastery and immediately one of the young monks ran the request two hundred feet higher up the small path to the abbot's cell. The three remaining monks were full of curiosity, asking Khenpo all sorts of questions. The most active and smiling was Namdrol, who would become our personal guide. Soon the answer came back that we were welcome to stay in the room where we were.

I looked around. The entrance was hung with a dirty, heavy, cloth windbreak, as well as a door that did not quite fit the opening. Namdrol explained, through Khenpo, that at night we had to close the door to keep the dogs out. I had noticed twelve to fourteen dogs wandering around the kitchen when I huffed and puffed my way to our room. The walls were covered with a mud plaster, whitewashed, or rather yellow-washed, with blotches of brown showing through. They were bare. The floor was of beaten earth and had a square table in the middle, beside a post that braced the only beam running the length of the ceiling. The ceiling was also earth, held back by lattices. The roof formed part of the path leading to the higher cells.

There was no electricity, no water, and no bathroom. The latrine, fifteen minutes away through a complex of buildings and up a steep path, consisted of planks extending over a cliff and a rail to hold onto while defecating so as not to fall. The water source was about twenty vertical feet above the latrine and consisted of a natural spring not much warmer than freezing.

Khenpo explained that no one bothered to wash, because it was so cold and dry that microbes never had a chance to grow. Also, it was better to retain one's body oils. As he spoke we were served hot Tibetan tea, which the monks sloshed around in a butter churn. I now understood why all the monks' robes were caked with dirt and buttered tea. A rancid smell pervaded. The only respite from the dirt was the maroon color of the garments, which helped disguise the accumulated filth.

One wall of the room was made up of a long, small-paned window from which several panes were missing. This side opened onto our "terrace," which was the main sanctuary roof. It was surrounded by a parapet covered with gargoyles, prayer flags, and incense burners.

The weather had cleared, and the sky was a very deep blue as the sun set. John, Khenpo, and I decided we would stay in the room while J.W. opted for the comfort of a tent and his own bathroom facility located by some rocks near the river bank. Word that Khenpo had returned spread fast among the community of 150 monks. He had studied at Drikung for five months in 1985 with the enlightened retreat master who had since died. Every few minutes another monk would pop into the room to pay his respects to Khenpo. They gave him khatas or some small change, which he was embarrassed to accept in light of their poverty and his well-being.

Supper at our encampment was a vegetable noodle soup. The water came straight from the river. I did not have the chance to drop an iodine pill into the broth. After a few more episodes of this, I realized I could not control the *Giardia* and gave up, surrendering to fate. In two days, the diarrhea was with us.

Khenpo had decided to stay with the monks for dinner, so John and I grabbed his gear along with our own and were driven up to the monastery. As we walked through the main courtyard leading to the stairs of our rooftop abode, we circled around a pack of snarling dogs chasing a bitch in heat. The monks paid no heed, nor did they seem to notice the dog and mule shit strewn along the paths and courtyards.

By the time we entered our room it was dark outside, and four small candles had been set out. Khenpo had not yet eaten. He was hunched over in one corner talking to an old monk. The tops of their heads were not more than six inches apart. John set up his sleeping bag on a pallet against one of the walls, and I decided to set up my bedding on the pallet along the window. I wanted to be near the fresh air coming in through the missing panes. My sleeping bag was rated at fifteen degrees below zero, so I would feel cozy. While John and I unpacked, Namdrol went to the kitchen to get the Chinese equivalent of a Coleman lantern and a pot of soup for Khenpo. The soup was served in a large bowl that Namdrol wiped shining clean with a filthy cloth. It was a gray-beige color, of thick consistency, with lumps that thumped into the bowl as Namdrol ladled it out. The soup was *tsampa*, barley flour mixed with Tibetan tea and a few lumps of yak cheese. Khenpo ate four full bowls while in animated talk with the old monk.

Namdrol listening to old monk talking with Khenpo.

Four younger monks hung about to listen and watch John and me get ready for bed. We indicated we wanted to brush our teeth. The monks all laughed but eventually brought two full thermoses, one of Tibetan tea and the other of hot water. We went out on our "terrace" and brushed our teeth under the stars. We rinsed our hands and faces and then hopped into the sleeping bags. Around 8:30 the old monk left and Khenpo set up his sleeping bag along the back wall. Khenpo led us in a short meditation and blessed the younger monks, who then left. By 9:00 lights were out, and we were all fast asleep.

Around 2:00 in the morning I had a desperate need to pee. I slipped out of my bag, put on my heavy polypropylene underwear, jacket, and boots, and creaked out the door with my flashlight. John was already outside, peeing down a waterspout along the parapet. Millions of stars were dancing in a deep, dark, blue-velvet sky with streams of cottony clouds flowing below them. John and I just stood there in the cold looking up, totally awed by the power and beauty of our surroundings. We both exploded into a laughter of joy, embraced each other, and headed back to our bags. Khenpo was snoring gently.

Next thing I knew, gray light was coming through the window and J.W. showed up with his gear. He announced he was joining us and that the truck had come up to the turnaround in front of the monastery. There, Tsedor, the cook, and the two drivers would set up a common tent. The cook was using the monastery kitchen, which was furnished with a wood fire and one gas burner. Our breakfast was a bland rice soup to which we added some of my instant oats.

After breakfast we proceeded two hundred feet up the mountain to pay our respects to the head abbot. His shelter occupied two rooms, each about eight feet by ten feet, plus a tiny cubicle for cooking. Khenpo sat next to the abbot on his pallet, while the rest of us sat on another pallet at a right angle to them. The abbot then gave us a teaching for the next two hours. He was a thin, stark, clear-eyed man who stared energy into me whenever our eyes connected. This was unusual; most Tibetan monks sealed their energy or operated above the crown. I suspected they sealed their energy much as the Taoists did: sending the energy out of the belly button in a counter-clockwise motion, upward around the body to about six inches to a foot above the head; then reversing the energy in a downward, clockwise spiral to a foot below the feet; then again reversing the energy in a counter-clockwise motion back up to the belly button.

The abbot had no right hand; it had been cut off by the Chinese during his seven-year imprisonment. While Khenpo translated, the abbot would lean forward, and pick up an empty mandarin-orange can covered with a cloth, lift the cloth, and hack sputum into the can. He would then put the can down and continue the teaching. He had tuberculosis.

Afterward, Khenpo gave us a tour of the relics, statues, and tankas of the monastery. We reached our room and were

Abbot's cell at Drikung.

served lunch: cooked vegetables and large, slightly warm potatoes. I ate heartily. I was trying to keep my weight steady, knowing that my metabolism was working overtime at these altitudes; my belt was down to its last notch.

Suddenly, over lunch, John bent over in an enormous sneeze. When he straightened up, he was in agony with back pain and could barely move. J.W. used various massage techniques on him trying to relieve the constriction, but to no avail.

Word came to us that the retreat master, who had been in seclusion for the last three months, had opened his isolation door two days before our arrival. Learning that Khenpo was in the monastery, he had invited him, and us also, to visit at his quarters. With delight we accepted and prepared to move up the mountain. His retreat was at the highest point in the monastery, about four hundred feet above us. John decided to stay behind; he was almost immobilized.

As we stepped out the door we were greeted by swooping ravens, playing on the wind currents around the terrace. In Native American medicine Raven is magic, and certainly there was magic in the air. High above the ravens I noticed large gray birds with tremendous wing spans and stocky necks, gliding slowly on the upper air currents. They were vultures. The sky was full of them due to the sky burial associated with the monastery, where the bodies of the dead were laid out to be eaten by the birds. Vulture was the medicine of death and rebirth, the transition of the physical to the spiritual. The Drikung Thil monastery had the largest sky burial in Tibet. I was told we would visit it tomorrow.

I daydreamed as we struggled up the steep path to the retreat master, but suddenly became cognizant of all the blue and purple flowers growing in the thin, crisp mountain air. We arrived at the retreat hut and were ushered in by an assistant who was always present for the master when he was not sealed in. The space was tiny and very dark. Khenpo sat at the master's feet, and J.W. and I sat across the room, only eight feet away. The small window barely illuminated the features of the retreat master. He sat cross-legged under his robes, as all the monks did; he was round as a Buddha with a very round head full of white hair. Even though the room was dim, I could see the sparkle in his eyes and his smiling countenance. He exuded love from every pore and compassion filled the room and all its occupants. His voice was gentle, warm, and soft as he greeted us and asked his assistant to make tea.

The assistant started a fire of yak dung, the prevailing fuel, in the tiny kitchen. The dung sent up an incredible amount of smoke (obviously the chimney was not properly vented). Soon the entire quarters were veiled in blue fumes and we could barely see Khenpo's and the master's silhouettes. Finally the master opened the small window and let in the cold, fresh air. The smoke cleared and we were soon drinking hot Tibetan tea.

The master then offered us his prize yak yogurt, which he had received that morning. The problem was that there were only two cups for himself and Khenpo. We were told to cup our hands, and the assistant scooped the yogurt into them, topping it off with sugar from the precious reserve bag. My hands were dirty, and I chuckled to myself as I lapped up the yogurt and sugar. It truly was delicious—thick and creamy—and I licked up every drop, including the dirt on my fingers. I was in another realm; nothing would happen to me.

When we finished, the retreat master gave us a special teaching that he singsonged to us without using any scripture. The loving and centered energy emanating from the master was so strong that I did not hear Khenpo's translation. I bathed in the glowing currents that ran through my body. My brain was empty, I was pure joy, and I felt as if we were pure spirit. At the end, J.W. leaned over to me and said, "This is it, Claude. This is how I want to live. In retreat, communing with heaven."

I did not answer. My philosophy was that we, as Westerners, incarnated to transcend the daily energies around us. I felt we were only to use these special moments to open our deeper selves for service to humanity. I came out of my thoughts, thanked the master, and offered him some money to help pay for the cost of those on retreat. He was most appreciative. We bowed to each other, my crown touched his crown, and he dropped a khata around my neck while giving me his blessings. He did the same for J.W. and Khenpo, and then we left. I felt totally spaced out. Magic was alive and doors were being opened.

Back in our room, John sat up and listened to our story. Young monks were again flooding our room, and Khenpo began to give them a teaching. We fell silent and I wrote in my diary. Khenpo's face was all lit up and full of joy as he taught. From time to time he would break into a giggle, as he was prone to do, his humor and heart following his teachings. The monks hung on Khenpo's every word. My eyes again grew teary at the compassionate scene of the teacher and avid students in this humble place.

Dinner came: a dish of *momos*, the best that the cook had prepared for the entire trip. Momos were large dumplings filled with either vegetables or yak meat. Having seen the meat market in Lhasa, I stuck to the vegetarian momos. Khenpo and J.W. dug into the yak meat specials. All the monks eventually left and we retired early.

I was awakened at 6:30 by the noise emanating from J.W.'s bed. He was doing his sit-ups, back arches, leg spreads, and bellows breathing, followed by a round of Tai Chi. Khenpo started his chanting, and so the day began. Breakfast was the standard rice soup to which we added my instant oats. Supplies were getting low. A few monks came in and held a talk with Khenpo. He told us that the monks had requested private sessions with him in the monastery, to which he had agreed. Afterward, all the monastery monks would come down to the main sanctuary hall and hold a tea ceremony for us. The custom was that we would pay for the tea and donate one *juan* for each of the 150 monks—a cost of twelve dollars for each of us. While Khenpo held his private sessions and we waited for the tea ceremony, I did Tai Chi, wrote, and talked with John and J.W. John's back was still giving him trouble, and he lay flat on top of his sleeping bag. He decided he would not join us for the tea ceremony, as any movement was painful, and he wanted to go to the sky burial that afternoon.

John also had a bad case of diarrhea. I developed an anxiety about my own soft stool, hoping it would not become full-fledged diarrhea. These personal difficulties

Tea ceremony with head chanter in light robes.

made me aware of my insignificance and pushed me deeper into my soul. As I wrote in my diary, I reflected on how Khenpo was guiding me deeper into the mysteries of Tibet. I knew that his plan was to lead me to a very special cave in the Drikung area of the Terdom nunnery. Khenpo had explained that to earn merit I would have to circumambulate the cave and its associated mountain, which would take the better part of a day. Each day that went by I felt myself drawing closer to that cave and to Yokar's statement, "You will shake hands with death." A slow, exciting tension was mounting within me, yet everything felt familiar, as if I had been here before and was retracing steps I had taken long ago.

At midmorning Khenpo walked into our room and announced that the monks were ready for the tea ceremony. J.W. and I joined him and walked to the main hall. The sanctuary was at least thirty feet high and had row after row of columns supporting the roof. Along the rows and in front of the columns were cushioned pallets where all the monks, except those in retreat, sat lotus-style, their maroon robes draped about them. Their shoulders were also covered with maroon capes, for the sanctuary was quite cool.

The head abbot, in yellow and maroon, sat on a thronelike structure. Khenpo sat across from him, slightly lower, but still elevated above the other monks. To the right of the abbott was his second-in-command and head chanter, also dressed in his best robes of yellow and maroon. J.W. and I sat on pallets off to one side so that we were positioned to see through all the rows of monks. Next to us, on an elevated platform, sat a stern young monk who, we learned later, was the head disciplinarian. He made sure the monks held the proper posture and did not doze off. Four young monks came in with large butter churns full of hot Tibetan tea. They went up and down each row and poured the tea into individual bowls in front of each monk.

While the pouring went on, I pictured in my mind's eye what the monastery must have looked like before the Chinese invasion. Eighteen hundred monks had lived along the mountainside. There had been many more main halls and hundreds of retreat cells. The monastery dated back to the twelfth century and had contained relics from seventh-century India. The Chinese had sold all the relics, objects, and statues to collectors around the world and then had systematically destroyed, by artillery, most of the monastery. Later, reconstruction had been done using ancient methods. I could not tell what was new from what was old.

The tea-pouring complete, each monk, on signal, picked up his bowl and drank. The abbot's chanter started the sacred chant, and all the monks joined in. Once the chanting began they proceeded directly from one sacred song to the next. The deep resonant droning through chest, throat, and sinus cavities vibrated through the entire hall and my every molecule. I was transported to my shamanic journey on the mountain knoll behind Ojo Caliente with David Carson,

*Author touching his head to Dakini rock, at sky burial,
with John and Namdrol watching.*

when I had heard and seen the vision of all these monks.
Once more, tears streamed down my face as I understood
I was being supported by the Most High in my innermost
self. I knew I was here for a reason, and I also knew I
would be all right.

The monks chanted to us for an hour. Another bowl of
tea was poured, and then they chanted for a second hour. I
was overwhelmed and borne beyond self. I had entered a
deep meditative state. I felt complete and accepted in all my
being. The chanting had shifted my perception: nothing was
required; there was nothing to do; I could just be. The tea
ceremony came to an end; each monk wiped his bowl and
placed it in the bag he carried underneath his robes. They
filed out of the hall, and J.W. and I rejoined Khenpo at the
exit. We stepped outside. In the courtyard was a tightly
wrapped bundle with a spherical shape on top. The thick cloth
wrapping was covered with reddish brown blotches.

Khenpo explained to us that the bundle was a corpse

for the sky burial, which we would visit after lunch. John was feeling better and joined us on the trek up and around the other side of the mountain. Also joining us was one of Khenpo's friends from a nearby village and his nineteen-year-old son, a monk. Namdrol acted as our guide. Because of John's poor mobility, we walked slowly up the narrow path. Along the way Khenpo explained that there were special "death" monks who handled the sky burial. The monastery received between two and fourteen dead each day. When a cadaver arrived the special monks cut sacred symbols into the dead person's back, then carved the body into precise pieces and placed the pieces on the sky burial rocks. Sixty to eighty vultures swooped down to make short work of the flesh and organs. When only the bones remained, they were gathered up by the pallbearers and crushed with tsampa (barley flour and tea soup) and water to create a paste. The paste was then spread on the sky burial rocks. Ravens and black birds arrived to finish the rest. Khenpo concluded his explanation as we came upon a pack of dogs near the prayer flags announcing the sky burial. The dogs hung out until the monks left, then rushed in to lick the rocks clean. Nothing remained.

The sky burial was shaped like a large teardrop and was composed of gray rocks ranging from one to three feet in diameter. At the head of the sky burial was a dakini rock about four feet high and oval in shape. A dakini was a female Buddha, or spirit, associated with good luck and the feminine qualities of receiving and allowance. The legend said that the rock came from India, and that one who touched his forehead to it would not reincarnate below the realm already attained in this lifetime. We all touched our foreheads to the rock. To reach it we had to step over some of the sky burial rocks not yet cleaned off; the dogs were still waiting. I was thankful to have arrived two hours after the morning corpse had been laid out. Few traces remained, except for those being finished by the occasional raven or blackbird. The prayer flags all around the site were flapping in the breeze, and the bright sun shone through the cool air. The burial monks left, and we remained standing there by the stupa in front of the sky burial.

Khenpo turned to us: "This is a good place for you to meditate on your own impermanence and death. Picture yourselves here, being cut up and eaten by the vultures. The three of you should sit on the stupa step facing the sky burial and meditate. I will go off to one side and talk with my friends. When you are finished, come and join us."

The dogs still stood off at a distance, waiting for us to leave. John, J.W., and I looked at the rocks. The energy of the place was extremely powerful, yet very settling. We sat down on the lower step and started meditating on our deaths. I first thanked the spirit of the mountain and sky burial. I opened my energy channels, then settled my mind and journeyed up a mountain, picturing a heart attack and my death. I visualized my body being brought to the monastery, cut up, and fed to the vultures on the sky burial. I felt my spirit hovering high above the rocks, watching the vultures pick my eyes and tear out my organs, pulling my beard away to get at my flesh. I then saw my bones crushed with tsampa and laid out for the ravens and blackbirds. Feeling calm and tranquil, I was an impartial witness to my own impermanence. The experience was wonderful.

I came out of my meditation and noticed J.W. staring wide-eyed at the rocks. John came to, and we compared notes; we each had had a supportive and insightful journey. Earlier, we had joked that when I died on the mountain the others would stuff me in J.W.'s large duffel bag and carry me home. John turned to me.

"Listen, Claude, now that we know about this sky burial, we can just leave you here. We won't have to carry you in J.W.'s bag."

"In all seriousness, that's okay with me. If I die on the mountain, leave me on these rocks."

J.W. joined in, "I feel the same way, in case I'm the one who croaks."

John concurred, "Okay with me, too. It's a deal between us—whoever dies is put on the sky burial. The only thing I have a problem with is that Khenpo mentioned it was the pallbearers who gathered the bones and crushed them with tsampa. I'm not sure I'm up for that chore."

We fell silent for a moment. Then I said, "I think if one of you died I could do it. I would crush your bones."

Both John and J.W. responded that they would also perform the task. We shook hands on the pact and walked down to Khenpo to tell him of our decision.

"Khenpo, could you legally arrange it?" I asked.

"No problem. Your body would be in Tibet and it would be perfectly legal. By the way, when I said pallbearers, I meant the burial monks. No one handles the body except them once the corpse is delivered to the monastery. So you can relax; you would not have to crush each other's bones." We sighed in relief.

Our party then climbed slowly across the ridge and back down toward the monastery to have tea at the nineteen-year-old monk's cell. As soon as we walked a hundred feet, the dogs rushed in to lick the rocks. On the way out we noticed a pile of yak heads and horns. They were huge, with spans of five to six feet, and had been left as offerings. J.W. asked permission to take one. The monks agreed, since they were not part of the religious practice but offerings in commemoration of the dead. I found the idea quite eerie, but J.W. took a full yak horn rack and put it across his shoulders. His broad torso and short clumpy steps made him look like the yak he was carrying. We rounded the top of the ridge and I checked my altimeter. It read 15,100 feet. No wonder my pulse was racing and I was short of breath! J.W. moved on steadily, keeping up with Khenpo, who would walk at full sea-level speed and then stop for five minutes. I just moved slowly and steadily. The group was spaced out, and John was slow and hurting.

We moved down into the monastery complex and passed the topmost retreat cell. I was overwhelmed by a calm, serene feeling. Tears welled up in my eyes. I realized the structure was the retreat master's quarters. I sat on an outcropping below his window and started to meditate. I heard the group continue down the path, and I entered deeper realms as the silence of the mountain engulfed me. I sat in ecstasy, finally emerging an hour later. Slowly, I focused on the deep blue sky, the mountains, and the river in the valley far below. I got up and ambled down the path. Around the next bend I met John.

"I waited for you. I figured that must have been the retreat master's headquarters even though I was not there the other day. I felt the energy. What a wonderful meditation! Come, they all went to that young monk's room."

We walked in silence, smiling at each other, then entered the monk's small room and joined the crammed group drinking Tibetan tea.

That night's supper was hot water, semicooked noodles, canned tomatoes, and hard, canned peas. TIST was not exactly generous with their food allowance, and we had three more days to go. We all laughed, and I was cognizant of how close a group we had become. Our spiritual journey far outweighed our physical hardships. After dinner all our young monk friends joined us in our room, where we distributed the clothes we had brought as presents. Our baggage was getting lighter, as were our bodies.

Breakfast the next morning consisted of cold potatoes and some salt; I had run out of instant oats. Khenpo got us some hot Tibetan tea and tsampa, which gave us some semblance of nourishment. Shortly thereafter Namdrol and the assistant abbot arrived bearing gifts, including a large yak cheeseball, a foot in diameter, which included a lot of yak hair. This was most precious, and we could not refuse. Khenpo later explained that we would give the cheese to the nuns, so it would not be wasted. We did, however, refuse a large butter ball, saying we could not travel with it. Each of us received a khata and a Manjushri clay amulet on behalf of the abbott and the entire monastery.

Each amulet's hollow core was filled with sacred relics, then covered with a glued cloth inscribed with Manjushri's mantra, *om waghi shavri mum*, "lord of compassionate wisdom in speech."

Manjushri was always depicted with a raised, flaming sword to cut through illusions and ignorance. I felt a close connection with Manjushri, for I believed having true wisdom meant occasionally using a flaming sword to cut through illusions—one's own or another's. Compassion did not always mean sweetness.

I felt very moved by the gifts, particularly since Yokar had predicted I would be given a small amulet to carry up the mountain through my trials. The pieces were all falling in place. Khenpo asked if Namdrol could join us on our journey to the nunnery. He had been to the cave several times and could be of great help. The assistant abbott agreed, and Namdrol picked up his small underarm bag and was ready to go.

12 Yeshe Tsogyal's Cave

Bite off the head of fear and make it your partner.
—Yokar

The drive to Terdom nunnery was through a narrow gorge. The Terdom River gushed along the side of the road. Small waterfalls splashed down from high cliffs, and scrub pines proliferated in the passageway. At 4:00 in the afternoon we arrived at the nunnery. The location was magnificent. The nunnery was situated at 14,600 feet among dramatically tiered rocks, its land forming a V between the Terdom River and a second, smaller river flowing through a tight gorge. A cleared knoll, across from the nunnery, was ideal for our camp.

The reality of the twentieth century and the Chinese occupation was brought to life by the plastic bags, open tin cans, and broken Chinese beer bottles strewn around the campsite. While we set up, Khenpo elected to climb to the head prioress' quarters and pay his respects. He also brought her our financial donations. Two of the many nuns who had greeted us escorted him up the cliffs. The nuns, in maroon robes and closely cropped hair, were also of the Drikung order. They all had very ruddy complexions and sunbaked noses and cheeks. They were small in stature and appeared to be in their twenties and thirties. I watched them carry large bundles of wood and food up the steep paths; they all seemed very strong.

Terdom was famous for its hot springs, so John, J.W., and I grabbed our soap, towels, and changes of clothes and trooped down to the water. The main pool of steaming water was enclosed by tall, circular stone walls that formed a large tub area. Soaking in the hot water with the cold air around us and the blue skies above was like being in heaven. As we soaked, a fat snake, perhaps four feet long, slid out from between the rocks and came down to drink. I watched its forked tongue darting into the water and thought about how my own power animal was the snake, representing the medicine of transmutation.

Khenpo arrived. "The head prioress is very nice. She has given us two rooms for our use on top of the main sanctuary. The sun is dropping fast, so we should move our things now and get organized for our climb tomorrow."

I objected. "I think we should wait a day, rest, get acclimated, organize the equipment we need, and go the following day."

J.W., drying himself with a towel, said, "Why wait? There is nothing else to do here, and we can organize tonight. You can't take that much up the mountain, anyway."

John concurred with J.W., and Khenpo continued, "The prioress said she could have four nuns circumambulate the mountain with us to help carry food, a kettle, a pot for lunch, and so forth. She will have three other nuns go up to Drong-Ngur Sundho monastery with our sleeping bags and small necessities. There is no road, and they cannot carry too much."

"What's Drong-Ngur? Are we staying there?" I asked.

"Yes, it's a very small monastery, maybe a dozen monks, at the head of a small gorge about an hour or two walk down from the cave. I think we will all be tired after doing the big mountain, so it will be better to stay the night there and walk down the rest of the way the next day."

John inquired, "Khenpo, what is so important about this cave?"

"It was Yeshe Tsogyal's, and she was Padmasambava's primary consort. She is considered the ultimate dakini in Tibetan Buddhism, an enlightened female Buddha. Padmasambava is the one who solidified Buddhism in Tibet. He married the old Bon religion to Buddhism. He made Bon deities the protectors of the dharma. Tantric Buddhism, as it is known today, is a derivative of the old Bon teachings."

I had heard all this before and was still not sure of the significance of the cave. I knew I would find out, though. I asked, "How long a walk, Khenpo?"

"Depends on how you all feel. Maybe seven hours. The prioress suggested we start at 5:00 in the morning using flashlights, so we can do the climb leisurely."

Something was not making sense to me. Khenpo did not sound clear about the time, direction, or difficulty of the climb. I did not want to rush. I wanted to clearly think out all that we needed to have with us. But I was outvoted. We would leave the next morning. We went to our rooms, where the nuns had already transferred our gear; they were like little angels. Khenpo and Namdrol took one room, and we three took the other. We walked down the gorge and back up the other side of it to the cooking tent.

Dinner consisted of the last vegetables in hot water with potatoes and salt. After the second mouthful, the food was cold. By the time we got back to the room on the roof, the sun had dipped below the horizon, and little light was left. J.W. had filled his backpack and was in his sleeping bag. John was hurriedly trying to figure out what to take. We all wanted to retire early, so we could wake up at 4:00 A.M. and begin the trek at 5:00.

I did not understand why the prioress and Khenpo felt we needed to start so early if the journey was seven hours, including the circumambulation, the visit to the cave, and the walk to Drong-Ngur. I decided to pack lightly. I stuffed a change of clothes and an extra sweater into a small bag that the nuns would take along with my sleeping bag to Drong-Ngur. In my backpack I put only emergency medicines, some granola bars, and in case of extreme cold or snow a pair of nylon Gore-Tex outer-shell pants. I went to bed. The time was 8:30, and I felt out of control.

The next thing I knew I was being awakened by J.W.'s exercises. It was already 5:00 A.M. I rolled up my sleeping bag and left it ready to be taken to Drong-Ngur. I filled my drinking bottle with hot water and some herbal tea bags. John and J.W. wanted the rest of the water, and the Tibetan tea thermos, to clean up their night defecations. Both had diarrhea and had used the downspouts. Hot liquid was needed to melt and flush away the frozen mess they had left. Khenpo and Namdrol showed up ready to go. There was no time for breakfast, except a cup of hot herbal tea and one of my granola bars.

After crossing the nunnery courtyard and the small bridge over the Terdom River, we started to climb a well-marked path. Within a half hour our eyes had become accustomed to the dim light, and we shut off the flashlights. The sun behind the mountain now lit the poorly marked path and narrow switchbacks. I had given my small backpack to Namdrol to carry; I wanted to keep all my energy for the higher altitudes.

I willed my heart condition not to enter my mind as a deterrent, yet I noted apprehension and tension in my body—and possibly fear. One of Yokar's statements came to mind: "Bite off the head of fear and make it your partner. Fear has great energy. Use that energy to accomplish what you want." And indeed, what I wanted was to reach Yeshe Tsogyal's cave. My inner will, my full self, had to be engaged and dedicated to this endeavor. Nothing else mattered.

J.W. and John had full backpacks and insisted on carrying them all the way. Khenpo had taken nothing and was climbing in his robes and thick walking shoes. I could not figure out whether John and J.W. were playing the macho scene or the martyr scene with their backpacks. In either case, I had advised them to go light, and their burdens were not my responsibility.

Four nuns were climbing with us, carrying lunch provisions, continually smiling, and giving us encouragement up the mountain. We were climbing the south slope of the mountain, which had small scrub piñon and grass, all frosted. There was no snow. By 9:00 A.M. John was exhausted and could barely move. He took off the backpack, gave it to one of the nuns, and put his left arm over Namdrol's shoulders for support. We talked about him going back with Namdrol, but he insisted on continuing. I personally felt that our pace was unreasonable. Khenpo led the way by walking very fast and then resting for five to ten minutes. This was contrary to all of my climbing experience. I slowed down to a pace of two steps to every breath and kept it steady, without stopping. That way my muscles did not cool down and tighten up but stayed warm and relaxed.

About midway up, our guide, Tsedor, caught up with us and passed us. He was not carrying anything and was used to the altitude. I checked the elevation from time to time on my altimeter and noted that it went off the scale at 16,500 feet. At this elevation I passed the rest of the group, who were needing longer rests. My pulse was 135 beats per minute, and I felt quite comfortable. As I climbed further and distanced myself from the others, I slowed down to a pace of one step for each breath. I judged the altitude from my last reading to be about 17,000 feet. The top of the ridge was in sight, and I could see Tsedor a hundred feet higher. The sun was now shining fully, the frost melting off the tundra. I felt that I was becoming lighter and my strength was growing. I practiced Vrill, Yokar's silent language, to call on my inner will. I also felt another presence with me: I had visions of the Dalai Lama giggling at me, telling me how my expectations had been worse than the reality. The closer I got to the top, the more I felt the Dalai Lama's encouragement. I heard him saying to me, "You see there is nothing so difficult, nothing you can't overcome."

Tears came to my eyes, and I started to laugh as my pace increased nearly to a jog within fifty feet of the summit. At the crest I found Tsedor sprawled out on the ground, catching his breath. Wanting to be alone, I continued up the ridge to a rock outcropping and fell to my knees, crying in pure ecstasy. I felt filled and surrounded with golden light, encircled by Chenrezi's ultimate compassion as manifested by the Dalai Lama. I looked around and saw snow-covered peaks in every direction. All appeared to be at eye level. I felt that I was part of heaven and that all was well with the world. A great peace and serenity filled me.

Khenpo walked up to me and sat down with a knowing smile on his face. The rest of the group rested fifty feet away. The air was cold and breezy. Although we were all well bundled with heavy polypropylene clothes and windbreakers, I suggested we not linger and allow our muscles to stiffen. "How far to Yeshe Tsogyal's cave from here?" I asked.

Khenpo responded, "We walk along the ridge here, then go down to a small valley, where we have lunch. The cave will be around the next mountain ridge."

"It's 11:30 now, more than five hours since we started," I said. "I think we had better get going."

He agreed. I was under the impression that the hike to the cave would be all downhill and that the hard part was over. I relaxed prematurely. The group started moving again, and it quickly became apparent that J.W. was in trouble. He could barely move. I convinced him to take his pack off and give it to Tsedor, who was empty-handed. After a few more steps it was clear J.W. could not walk under his own power. He looked at me and said, "My mind is there, but my body won't function. I'm operating on radar." We straddled him between two nuns, an arm over each of their shoulders. They laughed and giggled, carried him along the ridge, and then started down toward the valley.

John was still incapacitated. Namdrol had carried and pushed him up the mountain and was now helping him down the other side. Two hundred feet below the ridge, we hit snow and rock scree, typical of the north face of a mountain. The going was fast but slippery, and tricky. About an hour later we reached the little valley adjacent to a small river. The elevation was 16,400 feet. Tsedor collected water for tea and soup and distributed some chocolate bars while we waited. I was convinced the water would cause problems.

I turned to Khenpo. "All right now—where exactly is Yeshe's cave?"

"Not so far," he said.

"What does that mean?" I asked.

He turned to Namdrol and they talked in Tibetan for a while. Then he pointed to a ridge escalating off the north face of the mountain. "You need to climb back up along that ridge, pass a few peaks, and it is around the corner."

I suddenly realized that he might never have been there, and that from the way he phrased his explanation, he did not intend to come with me. "Khenpo, when was the last time you went to Yeshe's cave?" I asked.

"I never did make it. I tried several times, and each time, at this point, I was too tired. I still think I earned merit because I circumambulated the mountain in spite of not reaching the cave. The greatest merit is to do both—it is a very sacred place."

"Are you coming with me this time?"

"No, my knee hurts; I would not be able to make it."

"Khenpo, what makes this cave so sacred?" I asked.

"Yeshe and Padmasambava spent much time teaching in this area. Then when Padmasambava headed south to spread the dharma, Yeshe went to the cave to live. She stayed there for seven years and became a great enlightened master. People for hundreds of miles around came to receive her blessings and teachings. She is the greatest dakini—she is a sky-dancer. It is very important that you go there." He said this with a clear certitude.

"So who's going to go up to the cave with me?" I asked. "I don't know the way."

"Namdrol will take you. He has been there several times. One of the nuns can carry John down."

"Ask Namdrol how long to the cave and down—at my pace, not his."

Khenpo talked to Namdrol and after some discussion

turned to me. "Namdrol says four hours, maybe a little more, then one to two hours down. He says that if you insist on going, you should leave now."

"Jesus Christ, this is not what I expected," I said. "An eleven-hour hike that includes climbing twice to 17,500 feet!"

"Well, you don't have to go, you know," Khenpo said.

"That's true. But I didn't come this far to back away from my karma. Please tell Namdrol I would like to get going as soon as he's finished with his soup."

At this point I was handed a bowl of noodle soup. I knew it had not been properly boiled, but I needed some food, so I drank it with a cup of tea. I asked if either J.W. or John were in any shape for a trek back up. John responded, "No way, we're both dead. Why don't you wait until tomorrow, and we can all go up from Drong-Ngur monastery? I understand the hike is under three hours. We will all be rested."

"I don't agree," I said. "I think my muscles will be tired tomorrow. I am in shape physically and mentally to do it now, so I'm going. If you want to go tomorrow, I'll wait for you, but I'm going now."

"Suit yourself," was John's dejected reply.

I recalled that, according to Yokar's prediction, when my real trial came, all concerned would bow out and I would be alone except for a non-English-speaking companion. Namdrol asked Khenpo if I would agree to leave my pack behind. One of the nuns could carry it down to Drong-Ngur.

"No, I want my medicine in case something happens. Also the ace bandages, granola bars, apple, and nylon outer shell in case we get stuck up there. Besides, the pack might slow him down a little; he has thirty-two years on me."

John interjected, "You'd better have Khenpo explain to Namdrol what to do in case you have a heart attack."

"Nothing; you just put a few nitroglycerin tablets under my tongue, and if that doesn't work you deliver me to the sky burial. It's more of a mental security than anything else." John looked upset. I laughed and motioned Namdrol to move out. I grabbed two chocolate bars from Tsedor and handed one to Namdrol, which he refused. I started munching and walking. "See you all at Drong-Ngur this evening," I announced. And we were on our way.

We moved swiftly up along a well-defined path to a small intermountain valley. In the valley's midst was an abandoned sky burial about one-third the size of Drikung's. We stopped briefly at the stupa in front of the stones, and again I connected to my own death and impermanence. I felt alone but not lonely. I felt comfortable with myself. As we were leaving, Namdrol pointed to some rusty butchering knives among the stones, and in sign language, slicing across his arms and chest, indicated they had been used to cut up the corpses. Once again my impermanence loomed large. Namdrol shrugged his shoulders, smiled, and waved me on.

Immediately after the sky burial, the trail climbed steeply and became indistinct among the boulders and ledges. I continually motioned to Namdrol to slow down so I could reach him and catch my breath. My heart was pounding at over 145 beats per minute, twice my normal rate, and I started to question my sanity.

We reached the first peak along the ledge of the rising mountain. I looked down a sheer drop and saw the small specks of our lunch group making their way along the river to the Drong-Ngur Sundho monastery. In sign language, I asked Namdrol how far it was to the cave. He indicated the next peak along the mountain ledge and then made his index finger loop twice more. I was incredulous. I put up three fingers to question whether he meant three more peaks along the ledge. He gave me his broad smile and cocked his head from side to side to indicate it was no problem. My chest heaved for oxygen and my brain groped for understanding. My body self knew that it would perform beyond its physical limits; my monkey mind was not yet clued in.

We slowly descended along tough rocky crags to cross

I looked down a sheer drop and saw the small specks of our lunch group making their way along the river to Dron-Ngur Sundho monastery.

a scree and snowfield. Namdrol was in his maroon and orange robes and wore the Chinese version of high-top Keds, the flimsiest mountain-climbing shoes I had ever seen. He started to slip on the snow scree. He caught himself. My mind raced. What would happen if he went tumbling down the ledge? I had no clue how to get down. He caught his breath and smiled at me, shrugging his shoulders as if to say, "What's death?" I pointed to my foot and dug through the snow to the more solid scree below, indicating he should do the same. He sighed an "Oh." I had not done this type of serious mountain climbing since I was his age.

We proceeded at a snail's pace across the scree. Once across, we faced a sheer cliff leading to the top of the next peak. I tapped Namdrol on the shoulder and put both hands in the air to ask how we were going to surmount this one. He smiled and signaled that I should follow him. He started the ascent straight up, finding a crack for a sneaker hold and another for fingers. I could not believe I was doing this. It was clearly a situation calling for ropes, picks, and professional equipment, none of which we had.

I started up, placing my boot on half-inch protrusions and clawing at every tiny crevice. Each square foot of this ledge became my personal interest and laser focus. My heart pounded, and I smelled my own sweat. It was the sweat of fear, which had a different odor than normal sweat. I could not look down. My concentration and every muscle had to be focused upward on the small patch in front of me.

Yokar's words came floating into my head: "Bite off the head of fear and make it your partner." And so I did. I felt a click, or switch, in my head and in my body; I became clear and centered, with no hesitation in my movement and purpose. Fear became my strength, and I moved steadily upward with death as my partner. We reached the top of the second peak, and I collapsed on a rock ledge. Namdrol smiled and indicated we should keep going. I made the sign for time out.

My mind needed to rest. My body, already beyond its limits, was operating on straight adrenaline. I closed my eyes and again the vision of the Dalai Lama came to mind, gently chuckling and cocking his head to one side as if to say, "No problem, you can do it." I opened my eyes and Namdrol motioned me forward. We crossed another snow and rock scree and struggled up another rock face. I was using upper-torso muscles that were not prepared to support my weight on a continual basis. I had not trained my upper body except by playing tennis during the summer. I was amazed that I was able to proceed, and felt the only reason I was not at the bottom of a crevasse was because of forces beyond my monkey mind.

We reached the next peak, and again I rested. The Dalai Lama and Yokar intermittently swirled through my head. I was dizzy. Was I losing my mind? I got up and again moved on. At times, as we traversed narrow ledges, I realized I was not breathing. I felt as if my nervous system was not making my lungs draw breath and exhale. I consciously needed to force another breath, to draw oxygen from these rarefied heights. One peak to go. My last strength was being sucked out. My mind raced. What should I do?

*Each square foot of this ledge became my personal
interest and laser focus.*

How was I to resolve my situation? I looked for conclusions,
searched for outcomes. Nothing. My mind had nowhere
to go. I could do nothing except be present with the rock;
be present with death. My mind was short-circuited. I
transcended my mind. My inner will to survive and tell
the story was all that counted. As my fingers and feet
clawed at every inch of the rock, I felt new partners joining

me in my motion forward. The rocks, Mother Earth, the wind—all of nature was my partner on this quest. The universe was my partner—it was me. I was beyond death and life—*I was*.

We reached the last peak. Now the path lead down around a ledge to the cave. The descent to the cave included a partial chimney descent beyond my ability, but somehow I moved one foot in front of the other and did it. We rounded the last corner, and it was not a cave but a huge cavern that loomed in front of me.

The cavern was about eighty feet high at its apex and a hundred feet wide at floor level. Large ice stalactites hung from the ceiling along its entrance, like teeth guarding the entrance to a sacred site. One fell with a huge, crashing, echoing sound, reminding me to pass through quickly and with a pure heart. Inside was a large expanse with a very dusty floor. Prayer flags were strung across parts of the cavern. The wind surged up the mountain, flapping the flags wildly and causing small dust storms around the entrance.

Within the cavern grotto was a large ladder leading to a small cave, then a smaller ladder leading to a tiny space. Namdrol indicated that I should move into the upper spaces. As I stood there, Doug Taibi's words of Chenrezi came back to me: "The space you will find yourself in will be divided into three rooms, one large, the other two smaller. At this time you will only stay in the first one. The other two are for later initiation."

I thought I would follow the advice because everything seemed to be falling into place. I did not, however, have any intention of going through such a journey again. If I was to visit the other two caves in the future for initiations, it would have to be with my astral body.

Namdrol climbed to the higher caves, and I found a spot on a rock under a ledge to meditate. I felt totally at peace and had the sense of a warm female presence embracing me, as if large, soft, feather wings surrounded my body from behind. There was no explosion of lights, no great revelation, no astral travel. Everything was mun-

Author meditating in Yeshe Tsoygal's cave.

dane, familiar, old hat; I had been here before. As that realization dawned on me, I felt an internal struggle to remember. Messages were being communicated to me, but I was not hearing any actual sounds. I only sensed that I was starting to remember information and practices I had known a long time ago. I felt a quiet assurance within me that all would be revealed in due time. I understood that my old being had died or was in its final death convulsions and that a new octave of consciousness was about to unfold. I did not realize in that serene space that further lessons and tests awaited me at the bottom of the mountain.

Forty-five minutes had elapsed when I heard Namdrol come back down the ladders. We each ate a granola bar and split the apple. He showed me Yeshe Tsogyal's footprints in the rock, about five feet off the ground. I found the phenomenon fascinating. When she had reached a certain state of being, her body's molecules had become totally fluid and indistinguishable from those of the rock. Modern quantum physics would reach the same conclusion regarding the indistinguishability of matter.

I stood in front of the Yeshe Tsogyal footprints in wonder. Then I turned around and realized that the sky was fully gray and overcast. I pointed to it, indicating the possibility of snow. Namdrol nodded his head in agreement and made a motion to leave.

We moved out. It quickly became apparent that we would have to recross the two peaks to get down. I had been under the impression that the ordeal was over—that our path from here on was downhill. My mind could not process what was happening. It started to hail small pellets, which soon turned to snow. I let go, and my body seemed to meld with the rocks and Mother Earth. If I was going to die on this mountain, so be it. The ledges, which previously had been difficult, were now more complicated because of the slipperiness of the snow. My mind and will became bolted to every square inch of forward movement.

Somehow I found myself on top of the second peak, and then we started to move down. We reached a scree and slid down, then crossed to the opposite rock ledge, where Namdrol started to climb down. I whistled at him and shook my head and hand in the "no" sign. He looked at me, hands up, shrugging his shoulders in a questionmark. I pointed at the scree I was still standing on. As far as I could tell, it went straight down and did not appear to have any crevices or precipices along the way. Once, stuck on a mountain in the Dolomites late in the afternoon, I had slid down a snow scree and reached safety before darkness.

Now I indicated to Namdrol that I wanted to slide down. He smiled, shrugged, and put out his hand, indicating that I should lead the way. I began moving down, but the very small rocks and earth of the scree would not let me stand. So I sat down, both feet out in front, and slid, using my hands to slow the speed of the descent. The slide was an exhilarating experience—we both laughed hysterically. My boots, pants, bottom, gloves, and legs were wet from the snow and icy scree. The smell of earth and rock was wonderful. I wanted to merge with the mountain, with Mother Earth. We had a euphoric half-hour ride down the

Author starting to slide down scree to valley floor.

full length of the scree without mishap, except for a slight bump on my coccyx. Once at the bottom we could see the monastery, and we were there in an easy half-hour walk.

I was to learn later that there was a shorter route to the cave from the Drong-Ngur monastery. That path still included two peaks and a steep, 1500-foot ascent across scree, ledges, and other challenges, but it took six hours or so less time. In true Tibetan form, Khenpo had wanted me to do a complete circumambulation of the cave and mountain to earn full merit toward enlightenment. That merit would remain a point of conjecture, but my strenuous journey had certainly made me fully face death and all my fears.

On that mountain I regained full trust in my physical heart's ability to function, as well as full understanding of what Yokar called "volting." This was an alignment of more than 50 percent of the physical and subtle bodies (physical, astral, emotional, mental, etheric, and causal) in order to fully perform an intent. Volting involved the full commitment of the inner will or higher self.

13 Issues

For every surge on the side of light . . .

We entered the Drong-Ngur monastery and found the others ensconced for the night. Namdrol headed out to join the local monks. Khenpo, J.W., and John were all cozily in their sleeping bags on cushions raised off the dirt floor by wooden pallets. The room, small, dark, and dingy, was, as usual, on the sanctuary roof. The door was a heavy draped tapestry that lazily swept the dirt as the wind swirled around the monastery parapets. I stood in the cold, windy doorway and did not see any accommodations for me. The reality of having no sleeping mat did not immediately sink in. My energy was down, my mind was down, my guard was down, and my body was crying out for warmth and care. I crossed the room and sat on the corner of John's sleeping pad. I related my experiences on the mountain, the hardships, the Dalai Lama visualization, the exhilaration.

After about a half-hour of storytelling I could barely move my mouth. "I'm exhausted. I need rest," I said. "Where do I sleep?"

They pointed, in unison, to the mat on the floor in front of the drafty doorway. On this mat sat three monks paying their respects to Khenpo. Khenpo was in the position of honor, the most elevated sleeping quarters. His three-inch mat was underpinned by three wooden pallets, each about eight inches high, making Khenpo's sleeping quarters over two feet off the cold floor. "Thanks, guys," I said, with more than a little bitterness. Yokar's concept of engaging the energy at all times did not materialize; I still had a lesson to learn.

I was wet through and through, both from sweat and the elements. I was trembling with cold. I had let everything go, including my will power. There was no change of clothes; my small bag had been forgotten at the nunnery. I got out of my wet corduroys and into my pants shell, which was not in the least warm. I hoped my polypropylene long underwear would warm up and dry from my body heat. There was nothing I could do for my upper body. I needed to get into a sleeping bag. I was going to be fifty-five in a little over a month and I had no intention of dying after completing my trek to the mountain.

I was concerned about hypothermia. From my days of offshore sailing I knew hypothermia resulted when the body temperature dropped so low that vital organs ceased to function. Initial symptoms included shivering, an inability to heat the body extremities, disorientation, and the eventual loss of motor functions. My body was crying out for attention and help.

I said, "Listen, I cannot stay the way I am. I need to get into a sleeping bag to get my body temperature back to normal. Khenpo, could you ask if they have some small wooden pallets to put under my mat? Or, if you don't mind, I see three stacked under yours. If the monks helped, it would be easy to slide one out and put it under my mat."

"This is a small monastery," Khenpo answered. "I doubt they have any more pallets. I will sleep in your place. I don't mind; I have even slept in Indian railroad stations."

"Khenpo, that's unnecessary. Just one pallet from under your mat will do."

Nothing happened. No one moved. The three monks sat on my mat. J.W. and John chuckled. One of them said, "I guess you're stuck there for the night."

I was getting angry.

Khenpo repeated, "I will move to the mat."

Both John and J.W., from their warm, cozy, sleeping bags said in unison, "No. I'll move."

"For Christ's sake, no one has to move. Let's just get the mat raised, the monks off, and then I can get warm in a bag."

I was cold, exhausted, and shivering. Before anyone could react, Khenpo got the three monks up and moved his sleeping bag and pillow to the lower mat. He insisted I move to his spot. I was too exhausted to argue, so I took his spot and got into my sleeping bag. Suddenly things started to happen. The three monks quickly managed to find another layer and several large cushions to give Khenpo comfort. J.W. was asleep in his sleeping bag. I buried myself, including my head, in my sleeping bag in the hope that my warm breath would bring my temperature up.

Someone mumbled something about dinner, which consisted of cold potatoes and hot tea. No one offered me any, nor did I ask. I did not care. I did not move from my sleeping bag and watched the events with one eye from behind the flap. By 8:30 P.M. the candles were out and all was pitch black. My monkey mind raced as I contemplated ways of getting warm. I found some humor in my state; here I was in a safe environment, yet I was unable to receive help and correct my condition. I let go of my monkey mind and reconnected to my deep inner will, moving to get my temperature up. I started by bellows breathing, then switched to internal Taoist energy exercises. I did every internal fire practice I could remember.

By the middle of the night I had to pee, but I was too cold to get out of the bag. I held out for another two hours until I sensed warmth in my hands and feet, indicating my body temperature was back to normal. In retrospect, it seems the energy of my anger at John and J.W. helped the return of my body heat. My circulatory system was slowly redistributing the blood back to my extremities. At 3:30 I got up, put my shoes on, and by flashlight found the door, pissed off the roof onto the courtyard below, and hurried back to my sleeping bag. I could not sleep. My entire body ached, particularly my pectorals and upper arms. I had not realized how much work these muscles had done to support me on the mountain. I could not wait to get out of Drong-Ngur Sundho.

Dawn broke and we were served cold potatoes and more

hot tea. I had a potato. For energy, I needed something more—anything, but it was not forthcoming.

Slowly we rolled up our sleeping bags. I felt as if I were in a slow-motion film, my every joint and muscle aching. It took me over five minutes to get my sleeping bag in its cover. My breathing was shallow and my head drooped to one side as I shuffled forward. I crept to the outside latrine, two planks over a descending slope, gagged at the smell, and discovered a full-fledged case of diarrhea in addition to my exhaustion. By the time I got back to the room, the nuns had picked up all our belongings and were ready for the walk down to the Terdom nunnery.

I was pleased to get out of that hellhole. J.W. was fully recovered and suggested, "Do a round of Tai Chi to energize yourself."

"Hell, I'm lucky if I can put one foot in front of the other."

John said, "I want to go up to the cave out of curiosity." He thought he could go up the scree that we could see from our window.

"Go ahead, but you will still have to cross two screes and ledges, besides scaling two more peaks . . . and you have diarrhea!"

"The monks indicated that they go that way all the time."

"Fine, I'll wait for you," I said, thinking I really wanted to leave. John turned to Khenpo and asked whether he would join him.

"Sorry, I am too tired, but I'm sure one of the monks here could take you up."

Waving his hand in dismissal, as if to convey the unimportance of the cave and the climb, John said, "No, that's okay. I'll come down to the nunnery."

I felt that his attitude was whimsical. If he had the internal fortitude, he should do it, and not downplay even the easy route.

Namdrol took my small backpack, and our party, including the four nuns, started down the path toward the nunnery. Although it was a little past 9:00 A.M., the grass was still frozen and the sun barely touched the top of the gorge's south-facing slope. We headed down the gorge along the cold, swift-moving river, and within ten minutes I was behind the group and barely in sight. No one paid attention as they knew I liked to set my own slow, steady pace. But this time my slow progress was a function of exhaustion.

For the most part the path was downward, and gravity helped me put one foot in front of the other. When a knoll rose in the path, I had to rest for five minutes after each step of the climb.

Eventually I lost sight of the group and did not give a damn. I knew I could not stop and go to sleep because I would develop hypothermia. I also estimated that by noon the sun would reach the bottom of the gorge, and then my body would get some warmth. I could not believe no one cared enough to check on me. After forty-five minutes at this pace, I noticed John sitting on a boulder around the next curve. I was not sure whether he was waiting for me or had stopped due to diarrhea cramps and the call of nature. As I came up to him he gave me a big smile. "How are you doing?"

"Slowly."

He put his hand on my back, smiling as we both sat on the boulder.

"Do you think I can go to the bathroom around that rock and be out of sight?"

"Go ahead; ain't nobody around but us chickens."

He went, and then we plodded on down the trail, finally arriving at the nunnery around 11:30 A.M. The nuns had resettled us in our old room, which was cozy and faced the south and the sunlight. I crawled back into my sleeping bag and began to shiver, hoping once again to regain my body temperature. J.W., Khenpo, and John went down to the hot springs; I felt intuitively that the hot water would further drain my energy instead of warming me, so I decided to pass and stay in my sleeping bag. At 2:00

everyone was back and looking for lunch. John decided to skip it due to his bowel condition. I needed food energy and asked J.W. to help me climb the small hill to the kitchen tent. The walk was slow and painful in spite of my resting much of my body weight on J.W.. When I finally sat down at the rickety table outside, I could not even lift my fork. The only thing that felt good was the sun shining on my face. I sat there in a daze, not eating. J.W. helped me back to my sleeping bag.

I slept most of the afternoon while the group went back down to the hot springs. That evening I insisted I was not moving. J.W. brought me a bowl of soupy, tasteless rice that was good for the bowels but provided no energy. I slurped three spoonfuls and went back to sleep. I woke in the middle of the night, too hot in my sleeping bag. I was elated; it meant my body was back up to speed.

I woke refreshed at sunrise. We all walked up to the famous rickety table above the nunnery for breakfast, where we had to scrape frost off the table and chairs. Breakfast was scrambled eggs (I don't know where they came from—perhaps heaven), flatbread, and hot tea. By 10:00 A.M. we were packed and on our way to Lhasa, a slow, bumpy, six hours away. The air was heavy and tense; everyone was silent and in their own thoughts.

What a delight it was to be back at the Holiday Inn eating a proper full meal of noodles, chicken, vegetables, potatoes, and desserts, desserts, desserts. We all crashed in warm beds. After a sumptuous breakfast, we rested and recouped the whole morning; then we had a delicious lunch. Khenpo was under the weather with diarrhea and decided to sleep that afternoon. J.W., John, and I went to visit the Drepung monastery, the largest of its type still standing.

Drepung was clean, with trees, orchards, and well-kept rooms and kitchen. Many children—student monks— followed us around. J.W. and I handed out pens, and John the turkey feathers he had brought with him. When we headed back to the hotel I decided I would stay in Lhasa with Khenpo for the next four days while the other two went up to Namtsho Lake. At 16,500 feet, surrounded by 22,000-foot mountains, Namtsho Lake was said to be very cold. Khenpo and I were not in shape to go.

Back at the hotel, rather than wake Khenpo, I stayed in John's and J.W.'s room and talked until dinnertime. Almost imperceptibly, the tone turned a bit tense. The subject was compassion, giving, and expectations.

John said to me, "You talk about your experience on the mountain and your visualization of the Dalai Lama and compassion. Well, I must tell you I got angry with you when you came off your mountaintop. Saying 'Thanks, guys' the way you did when you saw the pad on the floor showed anger and expectation."

He explained that if I were really the compassionate being that I claimed to be, I would have given and not expected anything in return. I would have slept on the floor rather than letting Khenpo be degraded by switching places with me.

I was shocked, hurt, and totally taken aback. I felt energy drain out of me. "What does this have to do with compassion and giving? I was exhausted; I was wet and cold. I was probably near shock. Yes, I expected that you guys could've had a little consideration for my condition. I can assure you that if the roles had been reversed I would have had a comfortable setup for whoever came down the mountain."

J.W. responded, "I commend you for accomplishing what you set out to do; however, we're not all Claude Saks, who thinks of every detail and has everything neatly organized as you did for this trip. . . ."

"That's exactly the point," John cut in. "Compassion and giving should be acts for themselves, with no expectations in return. I was embarrassed for Khenpo."

I felt defensive and said, "He moved before I could react, and I certainly didn't see you make any move from your comfy sleeping bags."

"I thought about it. I really did, but it all happened so quickly," John said.

J.W. leaned forward from his bed. "Maybe the summation is that Khenpo loves you more than we do."

"You guys are mixing apples and peaches," I said. "But yeah, okay. I always used to expect something in return for my giving, whether from my kids, my friends, or the situations. I know I need to let go of expectations."

John picked up. "That's it—you must give from the heart. Giving is a one-way transaction."

I did not see how my organizing the trip and financing Khenpo had anything to do with the events of Drong-Ngur. Their attitude seemed to be coming from a lack of compassion, a lack of heart and sensitivity. Usually I enjoyed confrontations, but I was not up for this one. I felt hurt and angry. At the same time, I realized that my anger reflected my inability to accept the truth. I needed to let go of expectations and learn to engage the energy of my anger.

At this point Khenpo knocked on the door and told us it was time for dinner. We moved down to the dining room and tried to get Khenpo involved in our discussion. He would have no part of it.

"I'm a simple monk. I sleep anywhere and accept all that comes." And he bent his head down to his soup.

I was still seething after dinner and decided to take a walk. Khenpo was sleeping when I returned and I did not want to put the light on. I tried meditating with different Taoist energy practices to work through my emotions, but to little avail. Near midnight I again lay down to sleep but without much success. At 5:30 Khenpo sat up in bed and started his meditation practice. I felt a calm pervade the room and fell sound asleep. Khenpo had to wake me at 8:00 A.M. for breakfast.

During the night, pieces of the puzzle had fallen into place. I realized that John's open, warm smile and talk of feelings in many instances did not have active follow-through. He was stuck in his ego. As my Native American friends would say, he didn't "walk his talk." I also realized that my own monkey mind was working overtime, because

I was angry at John and at my own inability to express my needs without putting others on the defensive. At breakfast I was pleasant and calm. I decided I would make one point to John.

"I didn't sleep well last night. I was thinking about our discussion. I think the most valid point was about letting go of expectations. I've taken that to heart, and I'll work on it. The difference between you and me is that I speak truthfully from my feelings and I don't hide behind a smile. In my place you would have entered the room with a big Cheshire-cat grin and jokingly said, 'Thanks, guys.' No one would have reacted negatively, and you would have been helped. As you said last night, you always did whatever you wanted in your strict Italian home, because you did it with a smile."

John gave me his big-toothed grin and responded, "Perhaps I'm a better manipulator than you are."

"That's obvious," I said. "I gave it up. I speak from my truth, like it or not."

He smiled again. "Relax, I was only being facetious."

I looked at him, incredulous. "Right. Have a good trip to Namtsho Lake."

Breakfast broke up. I managed a perfunctory hug with John as he joined J.W. in the Jeep and drove off with the driver and guide.

I felt the dark side, both of myself and of others, impinging on my spiritual journey. Intuitively I was starting to understand that to walk on the path of light, in the reflection of the Most High, I had to be able to carry my dark side consciously at all times and still move forward. For every surge on the side of light, there was an equal and opposite surge on the side of darkness, for that was how the universe worked. This concept was reflected in the Tibetans' belief that deities were both compassionate and wrathful.

I reflected on the fact that no matter how high a mountain I climbed, I always needed to return to the realities of everyday life. I had incarnated as a person of the Western world and had chosen not to be an isolated monk; my destiny was to incorporate and transcend the energies around me, refining them in order to become closer to the Most High.

14 Completion

I just have an instinct for survival.

I was relieved to be alone with Khenpo. The next three days were wonderful. I relaxed and wrote notes on the Tibetan trip, and Khenpo spent much time with me reviewing Buddhist teachings and meditations. Our diarrhea was not improving. I had two remedies: Chinese herbs and a strong Western antibiotic. We split them: he took the herbs and I took the antibiotic. Three days later we were both feeling almost normal.

Our meditations transcended our intestinal problems. At the beginning we meditated on death and impermanence. Then Khenpo gave me a meditation that was a Chenrezi empowerment of compassion. I felt that this compassion meditation was a summation of the energies of Yeshe Tsogyal, her teacher Padmasambava, and all that the cave and my Tibetan trip represented. I also believed that the Chenrezi practice of compassion was an alchemical formula for furthering my vibrational change toward the Most High. Khenpo knew I liked to cut to the essence of a practice. He therefore kept the chanting and verbal teaching to a minimum. The main emphasis was on the empowerment, which was set deep within my being. No Tibetan practice was complete without an empowerment from a Tibetan master. This empowerment set the starting vibration in the self.

Following is a method for doing the Chenrezi compassion meditation as I practice it.

The practice begins by first quieting your mind and centering fully in your body. Then, visualize Chenrezi in an etheric form in front of you. The visualization should be as detailed as possible. Chenrezi is all white and has four arms, two over his heart; his hands are in prayer, flowerbud style. The bottom right hand holds a crystal *mala*; the bottom left hand holds a lotus blossom. He sits on a moon disk in the lotus posture. Study a tanka of Chenrezi carefully; then review all the details and meanings with a lama.

Once your visualization of Chenrezi is complete and held in your mind, merge with him on the etheric plane. Become Chenrezi. Picture a moon disk at the level of your heart, inscribed with the sacred Tibetan letters HRI. Then start reciting the sacred sounds of the compassion mantra, "Ohm Mani Padme Hum." Do from three to six *malas*, which consist of 108 beads each. Visualize compassion emanating from your heart to all sentient beings; the compassion rotates out from your heart in a clockwise motion. You may also do a slight variation that is more specific, sending compassion first to all your loved ones, then to all the people with whom you have had difficulty in one way or another, then finally to all sentient beings. Allow the compassion to emanate in waves from the place you are located to encompass the Earth. When the meditation is complete, feel the compassion of all sentient beings coming back to you and filling you. Then dissolve into emptiness by burning the visualization from bottom to top.

When Khenpo and I were practicing the meditation in our room in Lhasa, I felt very connected and yet incomplete. A year of Tibetan energy absorption would transpire before I would receive the fullness of the Chenrezi empowerment from Yokar.

Khenpo and I visited a monastery, bought souvenirs in Borkhar Square, and spent time with Khenpo's friend, Agon Rinpoche. I kept feeling that Agon knew more than he was saying, or else Khenpo that was not translating. I enjoyed Agon's company and invited him and his wife for dinner on the night that John and J.W. returned—Tuesday, October 6.

The dinner was very pleasant; most of the conversation was about J.W.'s and John's trip. They had a great time, although they found it rough camping in freezing weather with no shelter. The afternoon of their arrival at Namtsho Lake, the sun was out, a strong wind came in from the lake, and magnificent snow-covered mountains surrounded them. That night they both went to defecate and had a strange sensation they were not alone. Turning on their flashlights, they realized they were surrounded by wild dogs. Before they could wipe their rears, the dogs rushed in to eat the excrement, and John and J.W. fled. The next morning they awoke to a heavy snowfall. Tsedor packed up the tents and equipment in a rush. They got lost in the blizzard for an hour and experienced snow blindness, then they found their way down the valley to a small village and safety. Their experiences made for lively entertainment at the dinner table.

The next day, we shopped and went sightseeing. J.W. and John each bought heavy winter Chinese army coats, and I finally found a painted tanka of Chenrezi with Manjushri and Vajrapani. We had two more days to tour, including a visit to Samye and an overnight stay at Tsedang. On the way out of Lhasa in the land cruiser, Khenpo turned to me from the front seat.

"I forgot to tell you. My friend Agon was on a retreat at a vision lake above Terdom about a year ago. While there he had a vision of you—a tall Westerner with a gray-white beard who would come to Tibet and visit him."

"Khenpo, I can't believe you forgot to tell me. What else did he say?"

"Nothing, I did not dare ask further questions."

We visited Samye monastery, where I sensed a familiarity with the area. It was an attractive secluded retreat, but after all the special places we had experienced, was not worth the two-hour boat detour on the river. In the

Author saying goodbye to wrathful deity in last monastery visited.

course of the boat ride back, John grabbed me around the neck from behind, as if to topple me into the river. I nearly broke off three of his fingers.

"Hey, I was only kidding around," he said.

"Really. Next time don't choke me."

"You're still mad?"

"Maybe. I just have an instinct for survival."

I was still burning from being put in the wrong and

from the frustration of being unable to make my needs understood. Also, I wanted John to recognize his ego issue. Nothing more was said, and the tension simply hung there between us.

That evening we stayed in Tsedang in a third-class hotel. The town was not used to seeing monks, so the Tibetan help crept up to our room, one by one, to receive Khenpo's blessing.

The next morning we went to Yumbu Lagang castle, a replica of the original built in 217 B.C. and destroyed in the Cultural Revolution. Once the castle of the first king of Tibet, now it was a small monastery. Yumbu Lagang was built on an extremely sharp escarpment protruding from a mountainside. From this vantage point, the king could fully view and control the rich fertile valley on either side. I stood looking down from the parapets with an extreme feeling of *déjà vu* flooding over me. A question formed and repeated itself in my mind: "How does one rule with compassion and know when to use the force of wisdom to keep everything running for the benefit of all the people?" The puzzle felt familiar and comfortable, as if I had no hesitation to use the force of wisdom for compassionate rule.

On our way back to Lhasa we visited some small monasteries, whirling the prayer wheels as our goodbyes to Tibet. We went to bed early in Lhasa and were on the road to the airport by 5:00 the next morning. The departure was totally disorganized—suitcases piled everywhere, all of the passengers vying for an overbooked flight that left at 1:30 P.M. We were early and placed our suitcases in a strategic position for departure, then lay down on them. John took the opportunity to open up the conversation.

"Claude, why are you so angry?"

"I'm really not interested in rehashing previous discussions. I think my need as a human being in possible hypothermia overshadowed your silly concept of 'no expectations.' The simple fact is, you told me when you joined this trip that you did it for me. You were convinced you were going to save my life. What actually happened is that you dropped out, and your ego couldn't handle the fact that I'm eight years older and have a heart condition and yet made the trek to the cave."

"That's absolute nonsense." He started to rehash the situation.

My mind drifted off. I was tired and uninterested in any argument. I placated him and wondered whether our friendship would ever be more than superficial. We boarded the plane, took off, and landed in Katmandu. There Khenpo separated from us to go off to India. We all gave him big hugs of thanks. Our next flight was to Bangkok, then on to Tokyo and Los Angeles. The seat assignments on the last leg of the trip had us separated. I was pleased to be in my own thoughts, and took the time to write notes. About halfway to Los Angeles I got up to stretch my legs and passed the row where John was seated. I noticed he was crying, his tears flowing freely. The seat next to him was empty. I sat on the aisle armrest and leaned forward, saying, "John, are you okay?"

He responded with a sigh. "I feel Tibet has reconnected me to my innocence, to my core and joy of life. I realize how much I have lost that simple connection in my business and helter-skelter activity in New York." Then he shook his head as if to wave me off, and renewed his sobbing. I got up and returned to my seat. I later realized that I had engaged the energy around me but then had been unable to let it go. I needed to focus on myself. I had felt frustrated by Khenpo's lack of support for me and also by his ability, and my inability, to remain centered and calm. Subconsciously, I not only wanted to be recognized for having been wronged, I also wanted John to acknowledge his own ego issue.

Of course, at the time I did not comprehend that these issues were my dark side and that I had to own them as I walked my path.

I struggled with Yokar's statement: "For every surge on the light side there is an equal and opposite surge on the dark side, for that is how the planet works." Indeed, I had cleaned up my life. I had climbed my mountaintop, opened my heart, and endeavored to be conscious at all moments. Yet I was still bombarded by negativity. My dark side was keeping up with my progress to the Most High. Another of Yokar's statement flashed in my mind: "Embrace the dark side. You must embrace it fully and carry your darkness with you at all times so you can walk the path of light, so you can be in the neutral point." Slowly I began to understand what he meant. The more I suppressed my dark side or that of someone else, the greater was the dark side's manifestation when it surfaced. I needed to be conscious of my dark thoughts, to accept my dark dreams as the way my psyche was balancing my light side, and to acknowledge the presence of darkness wherever it surfaced. In so doing I could work toward a better self and a better world. I understood that if we could all fully feel our dark sides, we could walk the path of light and be in balance. Then Planet Earth could be peaceful.

I understood that the higher the vibration and the greater the consciousness, the greater the darkness that would manifest. I needed to be conscious of and feel my whole being at all times, to be fully who I was. If angry, I needed to be all of that energy, just as much as I did when I was in total joy. If I was totally in my body and expressing my entire self, other people would not be threatened by my emotions. In getting fully in touch with my emotions, I was also releasing them without outward actions.

The more I recognized my duality, the better I could navigate a path between extremes and become one with both. The issues in Tibet brought this to the forefront. I felt the issues, or energy, to be like the oscillating poles of a motor going from a plus to a minus charge— except that the oscillations were also moving into higher and more refined frequencies. Perhaps enlightenment was the collapse of the two poles into a unified clarity— clarity to walk that neutral path at all times, moving in the light, carrying my shadow as the vibrations moved up in octaves to a reunion with Almighty God. I needed to return to Santa Fe, be quiet, and meditate to develop my gnosis.

15 Understanding

All that counted was this very moment, no other.

Three days after my return to Santa Fe I had caught up with messages, paperwork, friends, and family. I felt plunged into a void. The phone did not ring nor did I want to see anyone. I was in a funk, alone, and trying to grasp the meaning of my journey. After meditating four hours a day for a week, I became impatient. What was to become of my life? I called Michael Morgan and asked to have a session with Yokar.

"Greetings to you from the Most High."

"Greetings to you, Yokar."

"How may we be of service?"

"On several issues. The first, of course, is, What was Tibet all about?"

"I think you know the answer to that question."

"Well, obviously, my lesson was to trust my heart, my body—to surrender to the life force and allow. Was this the gift 'beyond my human mind' that you were alluding to in Egypt?"

"Yes. Yet more than this, you disavowed your body entirely. To accomplish that feat on the mountain you needed full trust and faith in the Most High. You transcended your mind, bit off the head of fear, and made it your partner. You now know you can trust your physical heart for anything. No second guessing, no holding back."

"Tell me, Yokar, what was the mess that greeted me when I came off the mountain and returned to Drong-Ngur for the night?"

"There were several issues and lessons that involved not only you but the other members of your group."

"Well, I had particular difficulty with John, who, up to that point, I had thought was my friend."

"He is still your friend, but he has not yet fully worked through his issue—his ego. You summarized it well on your departure from Lhasa. He came on the trip because he thought he was the one to owe you a life, and he was going to play hero and save you. Quite to the contrary, he totally collapsed, and you ended up helping Namdrol save him. John compounded the situation by not helping when you returned.

"As for your personal lesson, it involved the question of need. Not only are you extremely organized, you are sensitive to others' needs and anticipate them. So you organized, provided, and controlled. For the most part, you have let go of control, but your need issue is still present, or it was at that moment in Drong-Ngur. You are unable to ask for something you need without getting angry, because it reveals your vulnerability. Your self-anger and frustration manifest in expressions of aggression. You put other people on the defensive. You try and shame them into providing what you need. You must understand that needing and vulnerability are okay. Christ was very vulnerable. He knew how to ask. When vulnerable and in need, you must ask, and you shall receive."

"Thank you, Yokar. I got it. What about this funk I'm in?"

"Stay with the deprivation—with being alone, eating little, and staying light. Go out into the wilderness— the high desert—at sundown and commune with your surroundings. Be alone and listen within and without. Listen to your guide, May-ling. She is an expert at deprivation."

Yokar had told me that I had three main guides, and one was May-ling. She was involved with the issues of my heart and apparently had supervised my open-heart surgery in 1977. Suddenly I had a flash of insight.

"Yokar, does May-Ling have another name?"

"Yes, many. She has incarnated many times."

"Is she Yeshe Tsogyal?"

"Yes."

"Why me? Why is the ultimate Tibetan dakini one of my guides?"

"Don't over-evaluate yourself. You have incarnated for a purpose. All of your experiences up to now have been building blocks; they have occurred to prepare you for your calling. Yeshe was available and qualified for your needs so she is your guide."

"What is my incarnated purpose?"

"You already know, and your task will evolve further."

"Besides helping with the Earth changes, will it involve teaching meditation and spirituality?"

"Yes, and much more, including teaching your old friends on Wall Street, as I told you in Egypt."

"I have no intention of going back into the fray of Wall Street."

"You won't. But after the changes that come about, they will need someone to teach them about cooperation and the new order of peace on Earth. They will listen to you and seek you out, because you were one of them and can speak their language."

"Yokar, that's a tall order."

"You are not alone; you will be prepared."

"So Yeshe is involved with this as well."

"Somewhat. She deals with your heart. You have passed the physical test. The next test will be your emotional heart, but we are getting ahead of ourselves. For the time being, meditate and spend time with yourself. A seed was planted in you in Tibet. Let it grow. Nurture its development."

"What seed?"

"The seed of wisdom and the power of compassion. Yeshe is there to help. Your being is changing."

"I'm overwhelmed."

"Don't be. You have much work ahead of you."

"What work? And who owed me a life in Tibet?"

"No comment. I have told you all you need to know at this time."

"Thank you, Yokar. Until we meet again."

"We extend to you the blessings of the Most High."

More than a year and a half would pass before Yokar would confirm that it had been Khenpo who had owed me a life.

In late November I finally came out of my long meditations and isolation from the world. I reconnected with people and started dating. I met Nicole through mutual friends. She was an attractive, dark-haired, dark-eyed woman in her mid-forties. Her eyes sparkled, full of mischief, ready for any adventure. Nicole was of French origin and had a similar background to mine. Speaking French together may have been our first attraction. Soon I was dating only her. She reawakened in me the feelings of my wild days in the coffee business. But I had doubts. I felt I was beginning to diverge from my path.

Although Nicole was not on a spiritual path, her interest and desire in spirituality were sparked as we got to know each other. I taught her some Taoist meditative practices that she embraced and performed faithfully every morning. This new relationship made me aware of my failures with Bette and the strain of communicating with my children. I felt that spirituality should encompass everyday life, and I was not clear about the outcome of the good time I was having with Nicole. I just felt a tremendous release after the tensions of my trip, and I went with the momentum.

During the second week of December, I received a call from John Paccione.

"Hi, Claude. I'm off to the Caribbean for Christmas and wanted to wish you a joyous holiday and a happy and healthy New Year."

"Thanks, John. I really appreciate your call. I was not pleased with the way we left our friendship after parting in Tibet."

"Didn't you get my phone messages? I called twice saying I really wanted to talk to you."

"No. I'm sorry. My message machine was on the blink,

and I haven't been answering the phone. I was in a self-retreat and deep meditation."

"Well, I called because I wanted to clear the air. I think we both had things to learn in Tibet, and we served as each other's mirrors. I feel very close to you and want to remain friends."

"I do as well, John. I'm so pleased you persisted with your calling. I want to wish you the best of Christmas as well."

Our conversation turned to old friends and catching up on each other's news. Both our tones were relaxed and congenial; I knew close ties were renewed.

Christmas was celebrated at Bette's house with the whole family present. We had been married thirty-two years as of December 22. I felt warm and comfortable, and realized how much I missed her. Our three children were there, and although they were cheerful, there was an unspoken tension under the surface. I had told them I was dating, and I sensed that they felt I had betrayed their mother. Explaining to them that Bette and I were locked into old habits that could only be broken by leading our own lives did not influence their views. Seeing Bette at Christmas, I realized that she, too, had gone through major transformative changes during our year of separation. I let the thought slide.

The urge to write about my Tibetan journey and my transformation was getting much stronger. I decided I needed to go to a secluded, comfortable, warm place to write. I asked Nicole if she would like to join me on a Mexican beach with the understanding that I would spend most of the time writing. In mid-January 1993 we flew to the Pacific coast of Mexico. For two weeks I wrote while Nicole swam and sunbathed, dragging me, from time to time, into the water. The weather was hot and sultry, and the warm salt water was wonderful after the cold Santa Fe winter.

Every night we went out to a different restaurant, drank Tequila, and reveled. Nicole held up her side of the bargain, and I completed 70 percent of a rough draft. When I was not writing, I seemed to be at a continual party. I wondered if this was truly the way I wanted to live. Although Nicole and I were intimate, I felt we lacked a certain connection, a certain softness of flow and emotional understanding. I knew that eventually my serious side and my need to be more consciously connected to spirit on a daily basis would surface. How this would manifest itself remained to be seen.

I flew from Mexico to San Diego, where I helped facilitate a men's weekend workshop. Upon my return to Santa Fe I came down with a stubborn case of the flu. My temperature climbed to 103 degrees and I was unable to break the fever for four days. Images of my life with Bette floated through my mind: Cruising together and dropping anchor in remote coves along the Elysobeth Isles of Martha's Vineyard Sound. Making love with her on board the yacht. The quiet lapping of waves against the hull as we fell asleep. Her spunk as a full-fledged member of the crew, racing with and against men in hair-raising situations, both in Block Island and Antigua. Our wonderful hikes and camping in the wilderness of the Southwest. The birth of our children. Her enormous caring and love.

On the third night of my flu, at 3:00 A.M., I wrote Bette a four-page letter. I expressed my love for her, my recollections of good times past, and my hope that we could come back together as new people. I said I believed that we had both changed and found our inner truths. I expressed my desire to see her so that we could explore the possibility of coming together again.

I met with Nicole and told her of my unresolved feelings for Bette. I knew I was hurting her, but felt that direct communication was the only way to be fair in the long run. I was saddened to see Nicole walk out of my life.

After a month, Bette and I decided to give our marriage another try. We wanted to perform a ritual to commemorate and solidify our commitment. On April 22, David Carson was to receive a sacred Choctaw pipe bundle in a sweat ceremony led by Night Chase, a Lakota medicine man. The woman who had inherited the pipe wanted to pass the pipe on to David, who was of Choctaw lineage. I was asked if I would like to attend. Honored, I accepted. I asked David and Night Chase whether I could bring Bette so we could renew our vows in the sweat. They agreed.

I went early and helped Night Chase build the sweat lodge, wanting to be part of creating the place of Bette's and my renewal. When I arrived, the circle for the lodge had already been cleared and the willow branches had been rough-cut. Together, Night Chase and I cut the branches to the right size—strong enough to be jammed into the ground, yet long and flexible enough to be bent and tied to the branches from the opposite side of the lodge. We used twelve branches in all, carefully spaced and bent to form the infrastructure of the lodge. We dug a fire hole to hold the red-hot rocks for the sweat, and then covered the lodge with blankets, carpets, and tarps. In keeping with Lakota tradition, the lodge's opening was to the west, the direction of the dreamtime. Night Chase and I then built an altar in front of the opening, upon which participants could place personal objects to be blessed along with the pipe bundle. A roaring fire was started in a pit a few feet from the opening. Volcanic rocks for the sweat, in sacred numbers, were placed in the blaze.

Bette arrived, and we all made our prayer bundles. Each person cut four squares of cloth, one each in red, yellow, black, and white. Placing a pinch of tobacco in the four squares, we made a prayer and wish for each bundle. The bundles were to be thrown in the fire after they hung in the sweat lodge during the ceremony.

The rocks were glowing red; it was time to begin. The men stripped down to cotton shorts and the women to plain cotton dresses. We were each sanctified by sage smoke, and after proper ceremony entered the sweat lodge. The sweat was to include four rounds of prayer, drumming, and song. Then we would pass the pipe bundle. Finally, Bette and I would renew our vows.

The ceremony began. Within a short time, I was sweating profusely and my legs and shorts were getting muddy from the stream of perspiration on the ground. I went deep into myself, appreciative of the occasion and the energy being generated. I reflected on the combination of people at the ceremony. The sweat was being performed by a Sioux, on an Apache friend's land, for a Choctaw. The fire tender was a Navaho, and one of the attendants was a medicine woman of the Hawaiian Kahuna tradition. The rest of us were Caucasians of various backgrounds. During the prayer round, I expressed the wish that all nations could come together in cooperation as we had for this ceremony.

The heat and the energy kept rising. Then came the time for Bette and me to renew our vows. My bandanna was soaked. Sweat poured down my face, into my eyes, and along my entire body. The words I had prepared prior to the sweat had evaporated with the heat. All that was left were words from my heart:

"My dearest Bette, after all these many years I can only come to you with an open heart. I vow always to speak to you my deepest truth, whatever the circumstances. I vow to be present at every moment we have together. I vow to love you with open heart. I vow to be compassionate and conscious at the times of our disagreements—for no one can guarantee us the future. And so I vow to love you unconditionally for whatever time we have together on this Earth."

The lodge was pitch black and silent. I could hear my perspiration dripping onto my lap. I could feel Bette's emotions before she spoke. I listened as her voice first quivered and then steadied:

"Every day when I drive to school I pass a very old cherry tree. It is gnarled and twisted from the high desert wind and the brutal sun, yet it stands tall in its majesty, and is showing new shoots and leaves. I see our marriage as this tree that has weathered many storms and has had its old branches pruned. Like this tree, I feel the spring upon us, with new growth and the hope of flowers to come."

We embraced in the heat and the dark. Our sweat mingled and we were one. All that counted was this very moment, no other.

EPILOGUE

Balance does not mean being static, for every-
thing in the universe is continually changing.
—Yokar

A year has passed since I reconnected with Bette, and we are still happily together. Our daughter Claire was blasé about our reconnection, for she felt we had never separated in spirit. Marc was overjoyed at our reunion and concentrated his energies on loving both of us as parents instead of supporting each of us individually.

Eric needed to adjust the most, for the unspoken chasm between us had been left unresolved. He visited Santa Fe and Albuquerque to show some of his video work. During the time we spent together, our mutual hurt flared into anger over a minor incident. We were in a small Italian restaurant at the time. I told him that I did not want to rehash our past difficulties but wished to use them as lessons for growth.

Eric put his fork down, shook his head, and said, "Dad, when you called you were angry. You barely said hello, and then you launched into my not sending you a birthday card or calling you. My feelings were split. I admired your accomplishments and the way you supported my path, but I was extremely upset at your abandoning Mom. And so, yes, I told you I would support Mom; that you were a big guy and could take care of yourself."

"Yes, I remember. I couldn't stay on the phone with you. For two hours afterward I cried. Eric, I love you so much, but I feel I have lost a son."

Sitting next to me, Bette was silent. She curled her hand

around my arm and extended her other hand across the table to Eric. He held her hand with his left hand and extended his right hand across to me. I took it and squeezed gently, the circle of energy closed. We all had tears in our eyes.

In a broken voice Eric said, "Dad, I love you too. You have not lost a son."

"I understand. I'm glad we could open up to each other." I knew that we had reconnected. We just needed to keep the dialogue open.

In March of 1993 I decided to have a phone session with Yokar. I wanted to understand more of what Tibet was about.

"Greetings to you. How may we be of service?" he began.

"Greetings to you, Yokar. I sense the energies of Tibet moving within me. My guide Yeshe Tsogyal has suggested I practice the Chenrezi meditation as taught to me by Khenpo. Any comments?"

"What is the reason for this?"

"I have difficulty with my dreamwork—particularly astral traveling—and Yeshe suggested the practice as a way of helping."

"Your difficulty with astral travel is your issue with control over your body. You fear the maiming of your body. Yeshe's idea is a good one. The practice will soften you, and perhaps you will come to trust that the life force will take care of your body when you leave. You must understand that astral travel is like death. Your spirit leaves your body. You have a strongly ingrained concern about your physical self. You have done much in-depth work to change your vibration but still have difficulty trusting that process. Your spirit is all that counts in the universe; your body is only a shell. Trust the leap. Your body will be fine while you are gone. Do the Chenrezi practice. It will ease your transition."

"Yokar, am I doing the practice correctly? I have a sense that the sacred sound 'HRI' is a type of Vrill, yet it is only used after the mantra 'Ohm Mani Padme Hum.' Any comments?"

"Yes, you are quite right. HRI is part of Vrill and has been distorted over the centuries. It should be pronounced 'hereii' subvocally out of the unnamed organ halfway between your heart and throat centers. The mantra 'Ohm Mani Padme Hum' should be used to quiet the mind and center into the heart before you start the Vrill. Then 'hereii' should emanate from the heart center as Vrill with a two-third ratio."

"What do you mean two-third ratio? Does the Vrill emanate from the heart as the moon disk revolves? Also, is there an associated color?"

"The two-thirds means that for every three waves of compassion you send out, you receive two from the life force—from the Most High. You receive these waves directly, not from other sentient beings as in the Tibetan practice. You become an energy conduit, or channel, of compassion, and this will soften you. The revolving disk is a good idea at first, as it will focus your mind, but you will find that it disappears as you become proficient. As for the color, you must understand that this is a very dynamic and powerful practice, so the color will also be powerful. Initially you will visualize green. It will start to become iridescent, opalescent, and moving. Eventually, you will find the green taking on hues of gold. Ultimately, it will become a deep gold with hues of green. These are the colors of ultimate compassion. I suggest you burn some pure cedar, not commercial products, and breathe in the fumes during the practice. It will help."

"Yokar, can I teach this information?"

"You have a resistance!"

"Yes, because it indicates that the practice as taught by the Tibetans is not complete. Yet, as you say, we have reached a time of no more secrets. This all feels familiar to me."

"The decision to teach is yours, for you are the one who will have to deal with any reactions."

"I feel it is my destiny, my karma from past lives, to teach the undiluted practices. This is similar to what Padmasambava accomplished. What does that mean?"

"You carry the same energy and vibration as Padmasambava. You understand how to take the essences of various practices and merge them back into a basic meditation, sometimes with a little help from the spirit plane. So you are an emanation, not an incarnation, of Padmasambava. You come from the same stellar mind. As I have told you, several stellar minds are working together, including my own, to accomplish the Earth changes both in consciousness and physicality. You are a resonance of Padmasambava, not a root cause."

"That is a heavy statement, Yokar."

"I told you, once you choose the path of the Most High, there is no turning back. The burden will be great at times, but you will be equipped."

"Can you tell me why I feel very close to Manjushri? What does that mean?"

"No comment."

I felt very connected to Manjushri and did not want to drop the subject.

"Tell me, Yokar, when did Manjushri incarnate?"

There was a moment of silence, then he replied in a measured tone, "Manjushri is not of linear time. He is of the past, the present, and the future."

"In other words, he was not a human but only represents an energy aspect."

"That is correct."

"So what is my connection to this energy?"

"You carry that energy. That is all that I am prepared to say at this time."

"Yokar, as I practice the Chenrezi meditation and become adept, will I be effective in teaching it to others?"

"You might be, but you must understand that most people will not be ready for it. They will be ineffective in their practice, for they do not have the power to project compassion. This is a serious practice that takes much transformation and previous work. You have the knowledge and personal power from previous incarnations and from this life's work, so you are ready to project compassion effectively. Others will feel your projection and may or may not be ready to receive it. It will be up to you whom you teach, and whether *they* will be effective does not matter. Any effort at compassion in the world is a blessing."

I felt exhilarated at the confirmations of my feelings; yet I was human and carried all the frailties of the species. I knew this was the beginning of my work.

"Thank you, Yokar."

"You're very welcome. We send you the blessings of the Most High. Good journey to you, my friend."

Everything comes to us when we are ready. The trick is to recognize the gift.

Bette and I traveled to Egypt in May of 1993 so that she could be initiated and I could become a second-octave acolyte in the Atlantean Karnak-Luxor tradition. At that time I also assisted Michael Morgan/Yokar in releasing all the temple spirits and spirit guards.

Ron Diana, an old friend and senior Taoist teacher, was also on this trip. Yokar had picked the two of us to assist Michael. Michael had to go to each of the holy of holies, enter into trance, and allow Yokar to release the spirit guards by Vrill. Ron's and my job was to catch Michael when he came out of trance. He would drop like a stone from his standing position when Yokar left his body and Michael came back in. We had been picked for our strength (Michael weighs over 200 pounds) and because Yokar felt we would not be negatively affected by the energy surge. From what I could gather, the spirit guards had been there for centuries to ensure that energy would be available for initiates and to keep out other disturbing energies.

We had two powerful experiences during the releases. One was at Luxor, where we felt such overwhelming sadness at the departure of the spirit guards that the three of us cried uncontrollably for half an hour afterward. The other was at Karnak. This temple had initially been consecrated for the intuitive or night or female side of initiations, but over the centuries it had been turned into a site for the practice of black magic. That was why Yokar had not used Karnak for initiations and had conducted separate trips to Greece for the night-side energy work.

Stellar mind wanted Karnak closed. When we eventually found Karnak's holy of holies, it was not open to the public. It was in the midst of rubble and reconstruction, and the smell of feces was overwhelming. The air was fetid and still, and it took all my concentration not to gag while Yokar released the guards. Yokar had to give me an extra burst of energy so I could handle all the negative vibrations of Karnak during the release ritual. When Michael came to, we could not wait to get out of there.

The releasing of the spirit guides in effect closed down the energy of the Egyptian temples and pyramids. However, they were still physically in place and open to the public. The energy lines of the Earth, the ley lines, had already started shifting in Egypt, causing physical and political upheavals, earthquakes in Cairo, and fundamentalist attacks on tourists. The Egyptian sacred sites could no longer sustain the higher vibrations due to the grid changes. Yokar later shifted the initiations to the Lapland region of Finland, where the new ley lines were beginning to emerge.

The Egyptian initiations dealt with the positive propulsive male side, or light side, of the life force. To be in balance with the life force, Bette and I also needed to be initiated by the intuitive, negative, attractive, female or night side. So we journeyed with Yokar to Greece, following the path of Demeter and the River Styx, to balance our night side.

Yokar once gave me a good analogy to illustrate how the life force works. At the time, I was involved with five different projects, all of them running smoothly, and I felt as if I were standing still.

"Yokar, I feel extra energy within me. What else can I do?"

"The reason you feel restless is that you are in the neutral force. All is in balance. You humans are not used to just being. You should be called human doings instead of human beings. When you are in balance, within the neutral force, everything will feel as if it is standing still. Your race has difficulty with balance. Remember, the life force is a triune force. The positive propulsive force and the negative attractive force produce the neutral force. Stay with the neutral force. Everything will continue to function well."

"That's easy for you to say, but how do I do it, Yokar?"

There was a slight pause. "You are a sailor and racer, are you not?"

"Yes, I am."

"When you are racing and you are successful, it is because all is in balance. You are in the neutral force, which is not static. It is a dynamic result of the positive propulsive and the negative attractive. The power of the wind on the sails is offset by the pressure of the water on the hull. You at the helm, and your crew, continually adjust the balance between the wind and the waves, driving the boat forward at full speed. Life is the same, with continual adjustment of the dynamic forces around you so you stay balanced, in the neutral force. Balance does not mean being static, for everything in the universe is continually changing. If you accomplish this in every moment of your daily life, you will have great joy, as when your boat is in the 'groove', as you call it."

In Athens, at the end of our trip, I got a deeper understanding of what was happening to me. I had a conversation with the master.

"Yokar, I feel changes in me—a greater clarity, a greater wisdom. And my heart is very open. As you know, Bette and I heard the ancient muses after the final initiation in the cave outside Delphi. Yet my mind cannot explain or encompass the changes. Are all the awakenings simply due to a vibrational shift? How do I understand that?"

"Hmm. Well, it is time I reveal to all the initiates what we have been doing. As you know, no spirit coming from the stellar mind can change your free will, for that is the universal law. We cannot tell you what to do but can only give you guidance and reveal truths. So to accelerate your growth and vibrational change we have, during these initiations, implanted in each of you the more refined vibration and wisdom of your future selves—your future incarnations. That was the only way we could push your progress without touching your free will. You will, therefore, increasingly feel that you are on the Earth but not of the Earth. You will see, feel, and comprehend beyond outward appearances."

I was stunned. I could not fully take in his meaning.

"Yokar, this will change all our perceptions!"

"Yes, indeed it will."

CONTACT INFORMATION:

Master Mantak Chia
Tao Garden
274 Moo 7, Laung Nua, Doi Saket
Chiang Mai 50220,
Thailand
Telephone: Country Code 66, City Code 53, 495-596
or 7, or 8, or 9.
FAX: Country Code, 66, City Code 53, 495-852

Venerable Khenpo Konchog Gyaltsen
Tibetan Center
9301 Gambrill Park Road
Frederick, MD 21702-1531
Telephone: 1-301-977-2228

Michael Morgan
c/o Stellar Mind Communications
8 Laurelton Trail
Flemington, NJ 08822
Telephone: 1-908-788-6735

Claude Saks
c/o Heartsfire Books
500 N. Guadalupe St., Suite G-465
Santa Fe, NM 87501
Telephone: 1-505-988-5160
Fax: 1-505-988-3214

GLOSSARY

Buddha Founder of Buddhism. Also a title applied to someone regarded as embodying divine wisdom and virtue.

Buddhism A religion and philosophic system of central and eastern Asia founded in India in the 6th century B.C. by Buddha. It teaches that right living, right thinking and self-denial will enable the soul to reach Nirvana, a divine state of release from earthly and bodily pain, sorrow and desire.

chakra One of seven centers of spiritual energy in the human body according to yoga philosophy. [Sanskrit *cakram*, wheel, circle.]

channel The medium through which a spirit guide purportedly communicates with the physical world.

gnosis Positive knowledge in spiritual matters, such as what was claimed to have been mystically acquired by the Gnostics (believers in a religious philosophy combining Christianity and Greek and Oriental philosophies).

guru In Hinduism, a personal spiritual teacher. 2.a. A teacher and guide in spiritual and philosophical matters b. A trusted counselor and advisor; a mentor. [Hindi Guru, from Sanskrit *guruh*, from *guru*, heavy, venerable.]

Hinduism Religion and social system of the Hindus, developed from Brahmanism with elements of Buddhism, Jainism, and others added.

Jainism A religion resembling Buddhism which emphasizes asceticism and reverence for all living things.

mantra In Hinduism, a sacred verbal formula repeated in prayer, meditation, or incantation, such as an invocation of a god, a magic spell, or a syllable or portion of scripture containing mystical potentialities. [Sanskrit *mantrah.*]

meditation Deep continued thought; reflection on sacred matters as a devotional act.

power point Location where two or more earth energy lines cross.

Shamanism Religion of certain peoples of northeast Asia and some Native Americans, based on the doctrine that the workings of good and evil spirits can be influenced only by the shamans (priests or medicine men and women).

Swami Hindu title of respect, especially for a religious leader.

Taoism A Chinese religion and philosophy advocating simplicity and selflessness. Developing the ability to flow with energies of the world.

transcendental meditation Practice that proposes to discover the nature of reality by investigating the process of thought rather than the objects of sense experience.

yogi Seeker of the Divine

Zen A Buddhist sect which seeks truth through introspection and intuition.

ABOUT THE AUTHOR

Claude Saks was a very successful commodities trader and the chairman of Saks International, Inc., the largest coffee trading
company in the U.S., when, in 1977, he suf-
fered a heart attack at age 39. After his recovery, he knew that in order to live a happy,
healthy life, he had to abandon his type A
personality and begin to walk his spiritual path.
Today, Claude is a practitioner of the Tao and
a certified teacher of Taoist meditation techniques and has been an active facilitator of
men's groups and workshops. His spiritual
work includes study and practice in the
Driklung Kagyupa lineage and the Luxor-Kar-
nak tradition. His articles have appeared in the
Chapel Hill (N.C.) *Sun* and *Body Mind Spirit*.
He currently resides in Santa Fe, New Mexico,
with his wife Bette.

HEARTSFIRE BOOKS

When we follow spirit, we are transformed by the fire of the heart, the fire of life. **Heartsfire Books** publishes the stories of people who are following spirit whether in their journeys, their healings, or their transformations. These stories encourage all of us to be in touch with our inner selves and to become more aware of the world beyond. **Heartsfire Books** publishes the message of spirit, the message of the heart. We hope our titles challenge you to go beyond yourself.

If you have a manuscript that you feel is suitable for **Heartsfire Books**, we would love to hear from you. Send a query letter and three or four sample chapters to:

Acquisitions Editor
Heartsfire Books
500 N. Guadalupe Street, Suite G-465
Santa Fe, NM 87501